KEYS TO INVESTING
IN REAL ESTATE

Fifth Edition

Jack P. Friedman, PhD, CPA, MAI, CRE
Real Estate Appraiser & Consultant
Dallas, Texas

and

Jack C. Harris, PhD
Real Estate Consultant
Crystal Beach, Florida

BARRON'S

Jack P. Friedman is a real estate appraiser and consultant in Dallas, Texas.
Jack C. Harris is a real estate consultant in Crystal Beach, Florida.

Friedman and Harris are the authors of *Keys to Buying a Foreclosed Home, Keys to Mortgage Financing and Refinancing,* and *Keys to Purchasing a Condo or Co-op.*

© Copyright 2010, 2005, 2000, 1993, 1989 by Barron's Educational Series, Inc.

All inquiries should be addressed to:
Barron's Educational Series, Inc.
250 Wireless Boulevard
Hauppauge, NY 11788
www.barronseduc.com

ISBN-13: 978-0-7641-4329-8
ISBN-10: 0-7641-4329-8

Library of Congress Catalog Card Number 2009036434

Library of Congress Cataloging-in-Publication Data

Friedman, Jack P.
  Keys to investing in real estate / Jack P. Friedman and Jack C. Harris. — 5th ed.
    p. cm. — (Barron's business keys)
  Includes index.
  ISBN-13: 978-0-7641-4329-8
  ISBN-10: 0-7641-4329-8
  1. Real estate investment. I. Harris, Jack C., 1945– II. Title.

HD1382.5.F75   2010
332.63'24—dc22   2009036434

PRINTED IN THE UNITED STATES OF AMERICA

9 8 7 6 5 4 3 2 1

TABLE OF CONTENTS

INTRODUCTION

Real estate has been the path to riches for many investors. In addition, it has provided security and income to retirees who had the foresight to build an estate. Contrary to some popular investment seminars and television promotions, success in real estate investing requires knowledge, capital, and the willingness to take risks. You have to know how to select properties, when to buy and sell, how to put together financing, and how to operate a rental property. This book will help you gain basic knowledge of real estate investment. It is designed primarily for the novice investor or as a refresher for someone who has been out of the field for some time. After you have mastered the material, you will be better prepared to understand more specialized books and articles on real estate.

The keys are designed so you can go directly to any topic you may be interested in. When a concept is used that is covered more fully in another key, the word is printed in SMALL CAPITAL LETTERS. When a new word is introduced and explained, it will be printed in italics. This helps you move around within the book. On the other hand, you may want to read through the sections. The key format allows you to read the book in short time segments, whenever you have a spare moment.

Section I will give you a feel for real estate as an investment and how it compares to other types of investments. The various sources of income are described. Major sources of risk are detailed. The section ends with a description of the essential stages of a typical real estate investment.

Section II explains various methods for analyzing property and markets to uncover investment opportunities. Even if you leave the detailed work to others, you will need to know what you want and how it can help you make decisions.

Section III covers the important role that financing plays in the investment. You will learn what to look for in a loan and how financing affects your investment.

Section IV deals with the keys to operating a rental property. Setting up an operating statement, negotiating leases, and controlling operating expenses are among the topics covered.

Section V concerns real estate investing opportunities with reduced participation, control, and risk. It provides investment ideas that allow more freedom from active management.

Section VI presents some important considerations when buying, selling, and developing property. Choosing the proper legal setup, using options, and deciding when to sell are explained.

After reading through the book, or before you start, you may have some unanswered questions. We have tried to anticipate these and have included questions and answers in Section VII. These are some of the most-asked questions in beginner investment seminars. They present a good overview of the subjects covered in the book. Questions and answers concerning market changes, including bubble markets, are also described in this edition.

We hope the keys provide you with the first step toward a successful investment program. As you proceed to enter the real estate market, you will discover the valuable services of various real estate professionals, such as brokers, appraisers, and lenders. While helpful, they do not substitute for your personal understanding of real estate investment.

1

INVESTMENT ATTRACTIONS

Real estate has proven itself to be a lucrative investment. There are many ways to invest in real estate and each offers distinct benefits. Nearly 70% of Americans own their home. This basic level of real estate investment frees them from dependence on a landlord and, hopefully, provides financial rewards in the form of appreciation in value. In addition, many people have acquired small holdings of income property. Often self-managed, these properties provide periodic income, some of which is tax deferred, and opportunity for appreciation gains.

Investors may take a more passive role as members of a LIMITED LIABILITY COMPANY (LLC), partners of a LIMITED PARTNERSHIP, or shareholders of a REAL ESTATE INVESTMENT TRUST or S CORPORATION. Through such entities, investors can own a part of large properties or diversified holdings. These entities also provide the advantages of professional property and investment management. Increased diversification can be gained by investing in exchange-traded funds (ETFs) dedicated to real estate securities.

Regardless of the form of investment, investors look to several advantages of real estate. Real estate often offers higher cash returns than alternative investments. In part, this can be attributed to greater RISK or difficulty of resale (illiquidity) associated with the property. Returns may be increased by using borrowed money. Real property tends to be a good hedge against inflation because rents may be increased as the price level rises.

Well-located properties may even beat inflation and offer resale profits from real appreciation in value. TAX SHELTER has traditionally been an attraction of real estate investment. Opportunities for tax shelter have been diminished by tax law changes.

In some cases, however, tax benefits still exist. Low interest rates can greatly enhance benefits from real estate ownership. Mortgage rates are at 40-year lows, under 6%, which allow investors to borrow cheaply. The investor can then own and control more property cheaply. When the property throws off benefits such as appreciation or cash flow above the interest expense, borrowing can be a highly profitable activity. The opportunity for existing owners to refinance and extract tax-free cash while reducing future payments has been a boon for many investors. So real estate has been a wonderful investment medium for many during times of high and low inflation. This is especially true for those who have capital reserves sufficient to weather periods of reduced demand.

Each of these attractions is described in greater detail in the sections that follow. Real estate investments cover a wide range from the relatively secure to the highly speculative. In general, the most secure investments emphasize current income production from highly credit-worthy tenants. Speculative investments emphasize appreciation potential from future developments. Estimate the amount of risk you are willing to accept, and choose an investment that matches that objective.

A key to successful real estate investing is identifying property that produces the type of income you need most, whether CASH FLOW, APPRECIATION, or TAX SHELTER, and acquiring that property at an attractive price. It is important to find property that is well suited to your needs.

2

INVESTING IN THE TWENTY-FIRST CENTURY

Investment opportunities are creatures of the economy. When the fundamentals of the economy change, investors must evolve to be successful. This is especially true of real estate investors because of the unique characteristics of real property and the markets in which it is traded.

Despite continuous change, there remain various ways for the small investor to participate and prosper. Real estate investing can get very complex, but one should keep in mind that it all basically boils down to providing usable space at a fair price to those who need it. The good news is that the opportunities for small, individual investors have never been better.

In the 1970s and early 1980s, the keys to success were knowing how to use tax shelters, capturing the gains of property appreciation, and using creative financing. Later these tactics became ineffectual as inflation abated, tax laws were rewritten, and real estate markets suffered under a glut of new buildings and falling market prices. The astute, as well as brave, investor needed to see the potential value of properties mired in a depressed market and have the staying power to hold onto the acquisitions until that potential came to fruition. This called for sound, fundamental management, based on the property's ability to generate rental income. In other words, there was a shift during the period from rewards going to dealmakers to rewards going to good managers.

In the early years of the twenty-first century, there was a return to speculative markets characterized by low interest rates and easy credit. The small investor was often overwhelmed by the "house flipper" looking for fast profits. The excesses of that period contributed to a major credit collapse that threatened to take the entire economy down. We are left with an economic landscape in which use of credit has been scaled back, through either caution or necessity. As the economy improves, expect the demand for all consumer goods, especially essentials like housing, to expand, though at a slow and halting pace. The small investor with a sound credit rating and a bit of cash can find opportunities in this environment.

The era of low inflation and limited tax incentives for real estate ownership continues into the twenty-first century. Fundamental value is still preeminent. In addition, the economy had become more globally integrated and energized by the phenomenal technical revolution made possible by the computer chip. These factors have brought changes to real estate markets:

- Asset pooling expanded the alternatives open to the investor. A whole array of real estate investment opportunities have opened within the publicly traded asset market. There are hundreds of publicly traded real estate investment trusts (REITs), which act like mutual funds that own real estate. There are even real estate mutual funds that invest in REITs and other real estate companies. You can get the benefits of diversification with better investment control by buying ETFs specializing in real estate. You can purchase shares in a specialized REIT that invests in one type of property or in one geographic area. Even more risk is available to those who buy derivatives—interests created by carving out specific rights from the total bundle of property rights. There are even securities available to allow you to short the market if you think things will worsen.

- Communication advances and lifestyle changes are affecting the way real property is used and, thereby, the nature and dynamics of demand. The full impact is unfolding gradually but has serious implications for property owners in the future. The opportunity to shop for almost anything on the World Wide Web may have serious repercussions for traditional "brick and mortar" stores. The opportunity to telecommute may have an effect on office space needs. A new era of frugality emphasizes getting value for money over luxury and conspicuous consumption.
- Real estate markets are becoming more efficient with the application of technology. Information that once was jealously guarded by real estate professionals is now freely available to anyone with access to the Internet. The result could be a drastic reduction in the costs and time spent in buying and selling real estate and a new role for real estate agents and loan originators. This will make real estate a more liquid asset, though still subject to a value that is highly vulnerable to its location.
- At the same time, owning property carries more liabilities than in the past. New laws place responsibilities on land owners for environmental impact and public safety. No property owner can afford to be oblivious of the provisions of federal, state, and local law.
- Real estate markets are opening up throughout the world. Opportunities exist not only in the developing nations of the Pacific Rim, but also in the formerly communist countries of eastern Europe and southeast Asia. A great and somewhat mysterious frontier for investment is opening in China.

The upshot of these changes is that there are more ways the individual investor can put money into real estate, and many of these ways overcome the traditional drawbacks of real estate investment, such as the difficulty to spread your investments over a number of properties and the ability to get in and out of an investment quickly. Today, there are four broad categories of real estate investment. While the big guys—pension funds and large international investors—are involved in each, small investors can participate, as well, and may even have some special advantages:

- You can buy and operate properties directly. The big investors have to buy large properties, leaving the rental houses, apartment houses, and small office buildings to the individual investor. There are tax shelter opportunities for property owners who materially participate. In fact, these markets remain the bailiwick of the small investor, who can operate profitably in areas of no interest to the institutions.

- You can buy shares of REITs and publicly held partnerships. In this sector, big organizations and individual investors may operate on equal terms. Public markets offer excellent opportunities for the passive investor who wants professional management to select and manage the properties. This is a rapidly growing segment of the real estate market.

- You can make loans for others to buy property. This has been largely the realm of institutional lenders and large insurance companies. However, there is a role for individual investors who want to provide financing or buy up existing loans. Often seller financing paper can be purchased at deep discounts. With commercial banks in retreat, you may find a good deal of demand for loans in your locality.

- You can buy securities backed by mortgage loans. Almost all residential mortgages and a sizable portion of commercial mortgages are pooled by organizations called "conduits" to serve as collateral for special bond issues. The individual investor can participate in this sector by buying interests in these "mortgage-backed" bonds.

In short, there have never been more ways to put money into the real estate market. As with any investment, you have to decide on your basic objectives:

- What form of return is most appropriate. Do you need current income? Capital appreciation? Tax-free income?
- How much risk you can tolerate. Do you feel comfortable putting all your money into one property? Do you trust someone else to manage the portfolio? Are you comfortable going against the crowd?
- The investment time frame. Do you need to cash out after a few years?

Whether you want to "get your hands dirty" with property ownership or want to put together a good portfolio of real estate securities, you will need to understand the basic nature of real estate investment. When the markets begin responding to economic fundamentals again, this type of knowledge will be even more important. The topics covered in this book will give you the knowledge needed to prosper in these markets.

3

RETURN ON INVESTMENT

Return on investment is the actual earnings from the investment. This is apart from any returns that represent repayment of the principal invested (return *of* investment). The difference is like distinguishing the fruit from the tree on which it grows. Both can be sold for money, but selling the tree provides a different type of income than would picking the fruit each year.

In real estate, it is sometimes difficult to determine how much of income is return *on* investment and how much is a return *of* investment. For example, if you rent a property that depreciates in value, some of the rental income must go toward significant repairs or even, eventually, replacing the building when it becomes useless from age or obsolescence.

Why is this important? It makes a difference in evaluating the performance of the investment. The return *on* investment determines how well your money is invested. Return *of* investment affects risk of capital. The sooner your investment is recovered, the less risk there is of losing it.

Measures of return on investment include the *equity dividend rate,* based on a one-year analysis, and the *internal rate of return,* based on a multi-year projection (*see* DISCOUNTED CASH FLOW TECHNIQUES/15). Consider that the rate of return you get includes these:

A safe rate: the rate you could get if you put your money into a perfectly safe, liquid investment, such as a federally insured bank account.

A liquidity premium: compensates you for the difficulty of and time required to resell your property. Stocks and bonds may be sold at market value within a moment's notice, whereas selling real estate may take months or years.

A portability premium: compensates you for the immovable nature of real estate. Stocks and bonds in publicly traded companies are perfectly portable. The certificates or accounts move when you move. But if you move away from your real property, management and owner oversight become more difficult.

A management premium: for the burden of monitoring and making decisions about the investment.

A risk premium: accounts for the chance that you may not get all your money back or that the return will be lower than expected.

You may use a build-up approach to evaluate the return on a particular investment. Consider a real estate investment that promises an annual return of 10% before taxes. You would hold the property for at least ten years. The safe liquid rate, as measured by the current yield on bank savings accounts, is 1%. The real estate looks like a superior investment. But don't forget to account for the premiums included in the rate.

The following increased rates are estimates that vary with the type of property, economic situation, and tenant or user: The real estate is not portable and is difficult to sell, so add another 3% for illiquidity. The real estate requires more investment decisions. Add 2%. Finally, there is much more risk that the real estate will deviate from the promised return. Add 4% more. The built-up rate is now 10%. Using these estimates, the real estate should offer at least a 10% rate of return on investment. If it doesn't, you might be better off with the savings account.

Real estate returns should be considered relative to other forms of investment. If real estate promises only a 5% return, and you can get the same rate from high-quality bond coupons, there isn't much reason to select the real estate. The real estate's illiquidity, need for management, and risk demand a higher return than do bonds, blue chip stocks, and mutual funds.

4

RETURN OF
INVESTMENT

Hopefully, any investment will provide a stream of future cash flow. A portion of this income represents the *return of* the investor's original invested cash. Any excess is a RETURN ON INVESTMENT. The return of investment may appear in a lump sum at the end of the investment term. For example, if you deposit money in a savings account or buy a certificate of deposit, your money is refunded when you close the account. In certain other investment situations, the value on resale is minimal or does not exist. In such a situation, the return of capital must come from the periodic cash flow stream. This means that some of the cash flow is a return *of* investment and reduces the return *on* investment. If you were to invest in a self-amortizing mortgage loan, the principal is paid down with each receipt. At maturity there is no lump sum receipt.

The return from a real estate investment is less clearcut. Whether periodic cash flow includes return of investment depends on how much is realized at resale. Consider an investment of $100,000 that provides an annual cash flow of $15,000. If the property is sold later for $100,000, the resale proceeds provide all of the return *of* investment and all of the annual cash flow is return *on* investment. If the resale is made for less than $100,000, a portion of the annual cash flow is actually return *of* investment.

Guard against investments that offer illusory returns. Suppose someone offers you an investment that provides a 20% return each year for five years. If there is no

11

resale amount, you will just receive your money back with absolutely no return on investment.

Likewise, if a property produces negative cash flow, all return of and on investment is pushed to resale. During times of rapid inflation, investors may purchase properties strictly for appreciation. The price paid is often so high that net operating income fails to cover debt service. In effect, the investor must invest new capital into the property each year. The hope is that resale proceeds will be sufficient to return the original investment and all annual cash flow deficits, as well as provide a return on investment. Be sure that the expected value enhancement is sufficient to cover the long wait to receive returns, with compound interest.

By contrast, if you receive high enough periodic cash flow, and then sell for a profit, the resale proceeds not only provide the return of capital but some return on investment as well.

The use of DEPRECIATION—TAX DEDUCTIONS affects the pattern of return. Depreciation claimed for income tax purposes allows you to receive some return on investment before resale through tax savings. If your property depreciates in value at the same rate as it is depreciated for tax purposes (resale price equals adjusted tax basis), all tax savings due to depreciation deductions is return of investment, not a return on investment.

In sum, in order to judge the investment's estimated value, consider the entire cycle of an investment (from purchase to resale), all of the investment returns and contributions, and their timing.

5

CASH FLOW

Cash flow is the money produced by an investment that you get to keep. Basically, this amounts to the cash, if any, left after all expenses have been paid. Expenses include those to operate the property and to meet all loan requirements. If income taxes due on the investment income are deducted, the result is called *after-tax cash flow*. Otherwise, it is called *before-tax cash flow*.

Cash flow represents the money produced by operating the investment. It does not reflect any appreciation gains that may eventually be received at resale or equity build-up due to mortgage amortization. Because these types of return are realized only in the future, cash flow is a measure of the current performance of the investment. For that reason, some investors base their decision to acquire a property on a simple *cash-on-cash* return. This measure is cash flow divided by the required equity investment. For example, a property that is expected to produce a cash flow of $10,000 per year and requires a cash investment of $100,000 has a cash-on-cash return of 10%.

The following is an example of how to calculate the cash flow from a real estate investment:

Total rental income if building is full (potential gross income)		$200,000
Less, allowance for vacancies and bad debts		– 10,000
Effective gross income		$190,000
Operating expenses:		
Management	$10,000	
Maintenance	25,000	
Utilities	7,000	
Property taxes	15,000	
Insurance	3,000	
Repairs	10,000	
Total operating expenses		–70,000
Net operating income		$120,000
Debt service (mortgage payments):		
Principal	$ 5,000	
Interest	80,000	
Total debt service		–85,000
Before-tax cash flow		$ 35,000
Tax on income from property		–2,500
After-tax cash flow		$ 32,500

A property seller or broker may offer a *pro-forma statement* of operations, such as the preceding, as part of a sales presentation. Be sure to review all figures. The rental income may be optimistic estimates rather than actual amounts earned by the property. Or, operating expenses may be based on last year's rates while property taxes, insurance, or utilities have jumped in the current year. You may have to recalculate the amounts to determine what you are likely to incur in costs or receive in cash flow.

There are various ways to increase cash flow. Check rental rates of competitive properties to determine if the market will allow rent increases. Rents can surely be raised when the space is full and there is a waiting list. Improving the competitiveness of the property, by remodeling or better marketing, may allow for increases in rental rates or reduction in vacancies. There may be opportunities for miscellaneous income from on-site concessions or parking fees. Operating expenses may be reduced by greater attention to personnel costs, careful use of utilities, and preventive maintenance. In general, attempts to cut corners on repairs and maintenance will yield short-term savings only and may affect vacancies adversely. Financing may be changed to improve cash flow. High-cost loans may be refinanced when interest rates decline. Interest-only financing may reduce debt service.

Expected cash flow can be an indication of how speculative an investment is. When appreciation rates are high, it is not uncommon for properties to be purchased with negative cash flow. The investor expects to have to "feed" the property (pay the cash flow deficit out of other income or capital reserves) until the property is sold. An expected large profit at resale offsets the years of negative cash flow. In other cases, investors may purchase properties with turnaround potential, those that are currently losing money but may become productive given renovation or marketing effort. These properties are expected to have negative cash flow for a time, but eventually produce positive income and resale profits. In any case where the cash-on-cash return is low or negative, the investment is speculative in nature. Eventual returns are based on anticipated improvements in market conditions or the appeal of the property and this introduces RISK that the improvement will not materialize.

TAX SHELTER may make after-tax cash flow greater than before-tax cash flow. This happens when the property produces enough tax deductible expenses to offset not only the tax due on the property's income but also outside income earned by the owner. Tax reform instituted in

1986 has eliminated most opportunities for significant tax shelter; tax deductions may reduce taxes on property income but not extend to outside income of substantial investors. Therefore, a real estate investor with a tax loss from properties may still be required to pay tax on earnings from employment, interest, dividends, and other forms of income. The amount of offset to the loss will depend on the type and extent of loss and the investor's other activities.

6

TAX SHELTER

One of the traditional attractions of real estate investment is its ability to generate tax losses. These losses arise from certain deductions and credits that reduce taxable income but do not require cash outlays. In other words, a property may show a loss for tax purposes, yet produce positive CASH FLOW. When this occurs, the loss is said to shelter income from taxation. Reduced taxes are a form of investment income.

Most of the expenses associated with rental property are deductible from taxable income. These include OPERATING EXPENSES and interest payments on the mortgage loan. Mortgage principal repayment is never deductible. (If the property is your personal residence, you may deduct property taxes and interest payments but not depreciation.)

Whereas cash business expenses are deductible for rental property, they represent real cash outlays. Therefore, they do not provide tax shelter. Deductions for DEPRECIATION (TAX) reduce taxable income but do not require cash outlays. Rather they are a way of accounting for the gradual decline in value of man-made structures. You are allowed to deduct a portion of the property's original cost each year to compensate for this decline in value. These deductions can shelter part or all of the income produced by the property. Except for high-income investors, you may also shelter income—up to $25,000 earned from sources outside the property—by showing tax losses of the property.

Although tax shelter has long been an advantage of real estate investment, it is very limited in today's tax environment. For properties placed in service after 1986,

17

depreciation deductions are based on a life of 27.5 years for buildings of residential properties, such as apartments, and 39 years for buildings of nonresidential properties, such as office buildings, shopping centers, and hotels. Land is not depreciable.

In the context of taxation terminology, *residential* applies to a dwelling unit that is rented to tenants. It includes apartments, duplexes, and four-plexes. When there is mixed use, such as a high-rise apartment building that has retail space on the ground level, the test is whether 80% of the gross income comes from dwelling units. If so, the shorter life (27.5 years) for residential property may be used. Depreciation cannot be deducted on a personal residence—it is only for business property.

For *nonresidential* property, which includes hotels, office buildings, and industrial facilities, a 39-year-life can be used. Many owners, however, prefer to use a 40-year life because of the simplicity of computation and taxes. A complicated alternative minimum tax computation may be applied if a 39-year-life is selected. The difference in depreciation is slight: 2.50% per year for 40 years compared to 2.56% for 39 years.

The amount of annual deduction is approximately 1/27.5 or 1/39 of the purchase price of buildings. In most cases, depreciation deductions under this schedule are too small to shelter the tax on income earned from other sources, such as salaries or interest. Any tax losses produced may be applied only against *passive income*. Basically, passive income is produced by rental properties. This prevents many real estate losses from offsetting income from wages, salaries, or other types of investments, such as dividends or interest earnings. If you *actively participate* in the management of the property, up to $25,000 of nonpassive income may be offset by passive losses. This begins to be phased out as adjusted gross income (AGI) rises above $100,000, and is eliminated at $150,000 of AGI. "Active participation" refers to investors who own property directly and make most of the investment decisions. The IRS defines *active partici-pation* as deciding on the rent to be charged, approving prospective tenants, and making decisions on major repairs. (There is a special provision that allows real estate professionals to treat rental real estate activities as non-passive. Eligibility requires the individual to spend at least half of his/her time in real estate trades or busi-nesses and at least 750 hours per year in real estate trades or businesses in which he/she materially participates. However, such a person might then be considered a dealer in real estate and lose their capital gain status.)

Even under these restrictions, depreciation does reduce taxes on the income from the property. In addi-tion, it may be possible to put together a tax strategy whereby investments with tax losses are matched with properties with passive income. The result could be a source of tax-free income.

An example shows how tax shelter is calculated:

ASSETS

Purchase cost of entire property	$1,150,000
Less: Land purchase cost	−150,000
(land cannot be depreciated)	
Building cost	$1,000,000
Divide building cost by depreciable life, in this case, 27.5 years, to derive annual depreciation. (or multiply by the IRS factor, which is .0364 per year)	36,363

OPERATING STATEMENT

Rental collections	$ 150,000
Less: Operating expenses	−50,000
Less: Interest paid	−85,000
Less: Depreciation	−36,363
Taxable income from property	$ −21,363

Because the income is negative, the property provides over $21,000 of tax shelter to be applied against income from other passive investments. Any unused losses may be carried forward to future tax years.

As a special incentive, the tax code sometimes provides tax credits for certain types of investment expenses. Credits are applied directly against taxes owed rather than as deductions against income.

Low-income housing tax credits (LIHTC) are available for investors who build, renovate, or purchase housing for low-income tenants. For newly constructed projects, a credit equal to 9% of construction cost is provided each year for a term of ten years. Substantial rehabilitation and acquisition receive a 3–4% annual credit. These programs are coordinated with state housing agencies.

Investment tax credits may be available for 20% of qualified rehabilitation expenses (QRE) of certified historic structures, and for 10% of qualified rehabilitation expenses of structures placed in service before 1936 that are not certified historic structures. There are numerous tests applied for qualification, so check with your tax advisor for details.

7

DEPRECIATION— TAX DEDUCTIONS

A key to real estate investments is depreciation claimed for federal income tax purposes. The Internal Revenue Service allows an owner of business or investment property to claim depreciation as a business expense, even when the property increases in value. Land is considered to have an unlimited life span, so depreciation cannot be claimed on it. Appliances, carpets, and furniture can be depreciated over a relatively short life, and buildings over a longer period. The exact life to be used has changed frequently. Almost every time the tax law has changed in recent years, the depreciable life has been changed. Usually, tax law changes affect new owners, whereas present owners continue the depreciable life with which they started.

Depreciation allows a tax deduction without the owner paying for it in cash. This gives the owner the best possible benefit—a tax deduction that doesn't reduce cash flow. For example, suppose an investor buys a small building for $1,000,000 and is allowed a 27.5-year depreciable life with the straight-line method. (The $1,000,000 in this example is for the cost of the building only. Any amount paid for the land is not depreciable.) The owner may claim a tax deduction of $36,400 annually each year (the first year is less depending on the month acquired). This deduction reduces the owner's taxable income, which will save income taxes. Yet, the deduction was created merely by a bookkeeping entry, and can be claimed even though the property rises in value. Thus the owner gains by reducing income taxes while the property provides cash flow from rents and would otherwise generate taxable income.

However, the taxpayer must be prepared to return the benefits received from depreciation when the property is sold. There is a concept called *basis*, the point from which gain or loss is measured. In general, basis begins as the price paid for the property. As you claim depreciation as a tax deduction, you reduce the basis. This increases the gain when property is sold. If the investment remains the same or rises in value, all of the depreciation becomes taxable as a gain when sold. In this way, depreciation that was claimed while owning the property generates taxable gain on a sale, unless the property actually loses value more quickly than the investor depreciates it on his/her income tax return.

Tax depreciation should not be confused with an actual reduction or loss in value. Tax depreciation does not measure the actual loss in value of property sustained in a year. It is an arbitrary deduction allowed by tax law.

In sum, depreciation claimed for tax purposes allows the investor to save taxes, but perhaps pay them back later. It is not a measure of a property's loss in value.

Recovery Percentages for Residential Rental Property
27½ Year Life

Month Placed In Service

Year	1	2	3	4	5	6	7	8	9	10	11	12
1	3.48	3.18	2.88	2.58	2.27	1.97	1.67	1.36	1.06	.76	.45	.15
2–27	3.64	3.64	3.64	3.64	3.64	3.64	3.64	3.64	3.64	3.64	3.64	3.64
28	1.88	2.18	2.48	2.78	3.09	3.39	3.64	3.64	3.64	3.64	3.64	3.64
29	-0-	-0-	-0-	-0-	-0-	-0-	.05	.36	.66	.96	1.27	1.57

Recovery Percentages for Nonresidential Real Property
39 Year Life

Month Placed In Service

Year	1	2	3	4	5	6	7	8	9	10	11	12
1	2.46	2.25	2.03	1.82	1.61	1.39	1.18	.96	.75	.53	.32	.11
2–39	2.56	2.56	2.56	2.56	2.56	2.56	2.56	2.56	2.56	2.56	2.56	2.56

8

TAXABLE GAINS

A *taxable gain* tax in real estate results when a property held for investment, a property used for business, or a personal residence is sold for an amount greater than its *adjusted basis*. Adjusted basis is original cost adjusted for DEPRECIATION (TAX) and capital improvements. In essence, a taxable gain is the taxable profit realized in a sale. A seller can have a large taxable gain from a sale, yet receive little or no money from the sale. Taxable gains are taxable income to the seller, and they are reported on Schedule D of Form 1040 by an individual investor. A portion of the taxable gain may be taxed as *capital gains* (that is, at a lower rate than ordinary income), some may be ordinary income, and some may be taxed at a maximum rate in between capital gains and ordinary income tax rates.

The tax rate on *long-term capital gains* is generally 15%, but it can be as low as 5%. A minimum 12-month holding period is necessary to achieve a long-term capital gain. Real estate used in a trade or business, though technically a Section 1250 asset, might qualify for more favorable treatment than ordinary income, but recaptured depreciation may be taxed at a higher rate than a long-term capital gain. So it is advisable to consult a tax expert when you plan to sell investment real estate.

Taxes on accrued appreciation are not due until the gains are realized. In other words, a property that is appreciating in value does not trigger a tax liability on the value increase until it is sold. This allows you to defer taxes until a sale is completed. However, there are two problems with this strategy. First, if property experiences a great deal of appreciation, the taxable gain will be large and may push you into a higher tax bracket. Second, gains that are due largely to inflation are taxed as if they were real income. If the property is held during a period of high inflation, a substantial tax could result. This is not unique to real estate.

With income-producing real estate, tax deductions taken as straight-line depreciation are generally taxed upon a property sale at a favorable rate. There are important exceptions, especially when accelerated depreciation has been taken. Depreciation tax deductions directly reduce the adjusted tax basis of the property. Taxable gains are calculated as follows:

	Original cost
+	Acquisition costs
+	Capital improvements
−	Depreciation taken
=	Adjusted basis

	Sales price
−	Sales expenses
−	Adjusted basis
=	Taxable gain

A property could be sold for the same amount as its original purchase and still generate a taxable gain. This may leave the investor with a tax liability and no cash to pay it. For example, suppose you face foreclosure on a property that was purchased for $1,000,000 with a mortgage loan of $850,000. Over the years, a total of $400,000 has been claimed in depreciation expenses. The lender forecloses and acquires the property for the $850,000 loan balance. (The loan was not amortized.) You get no cash from the sale. The adjusted basis of the property is $600,000,[1] leaving you with a taxable gain of

---

[1] $1,000,000 original cost minus $400,000 accumulated depreciation equals $600,000.

$250,000,[2] even though you received no cash from the transaction. This is called *phantom income*.

Taxes on gains may be deferred or avoided by several methods. If the property is sold in an *installment sale* (payments are spread over more than one year), taxes on the gain are paid at a prorated amount as principal payments are received. This may prevent a large gain from pushing you into a higher tax bracket. A second method is that property may be exchanged for "like-kind" property under Section 1031 (*see* EXCHANGES/53) and all or a portion of the gain deferred. Property passed to heirs will have its basis stepped up to current market value, thereby wiping out any accumulated tax liability on past appreciation in value. If certain conditions are met, the sale of one's principal residence is not taxed on up to $250,000 of gain ($500,000 for married couples).

A capital loss may be used to offset capital gains in the same year. If capital losses exceed capital gains, an individual may offset up to $3,000 of the loss against ordinary income and carry forward the unused loss. Selling a principal residence at a loss is not deductible, but a loss on the sale of real estate used in a business can be fully deductible under Section 1231 of the *U.S. Internal Revenue Code*.

Under present tax law, capital gains escape income taxation upon death. However, upon death the value of the property may be subject to an estate tax as of the date of death or, if less, an alternative value six months later. The estate tax must be paid regardless of whether the heirs sell, though postponements are allowed for farms or closely held businesses that meet certain tests.

---

[2]$850,000 loan balance is deemed to be the selling price, minus $600,000 adjusted tax basis equals $250,000 taxable gain.

9

INFLATION AND APPRECIATION

Inflation is the decline in the purchasing power of the dollar over time. Investors are concerned about the effects of inflation because an investment's real value can be eroded substantially by high or persistent inflation. When inflation rates are high, investors acquire inflation hedges such as gold and other tangible assets. Most real estate is considered a good inflation hedge. This means the value of tangible real property tends to rise with inflation, and minimizes losses due to deteriorating dollar value.

Appreciation is the rate at which the value of property increases over time. A portion of appreciation may be due to inflation. As general prices rise, so should the income from real property, just as a ship stays afloat no matter how high the water level. This tends to maintain the real value of the property. However, properties may rise in value even in the absence of inflation. A desirable location, a well-conceived project, population growth in excess of new construction activity, and good property management contribute to appreciation in property value.

Like any other investment asset, appreciation is greatest when favorable, but unanticipated, events occur after the property is purchased. If you are looking for appreciation potential, look for properties offered at bargain prices. Bargains may exist because of a temporary downturn in the market, a location that is currently out of favor, or an owner who is anxious to sell. Some properties in unattractive physical condition may offer opportunities for improving value through prudent renovation. In addition, undeveloped or unoccupied properties offer higher appreciation potential than do completed, fully occupied buildings. You must believe that you can turn the project around and make it profitable or that something will occur to make the property more attractive. For example, undeveloped land may benefit from expansion of an urban area in its direction. Some investors speculate on development around proposed public works projects to improve property values.

Appreciation may also occur in mature, conservative properties. As long as the property remains competitive in the market, its value can increase. Therefore, returns from appreciation can be expected in many sound real estate investments without risky speculation or property turnaround strategies. In these cases, appreciation will tend to offset inflation, allowing you to enjoy the periodic CASH FLOW from the project as a real RETURN ON INVESTMENT.

The effect of appreciation on investment return is increased by the use of LEVERAGE, which is borrowed money. In most cases, any increases in value belong to the equity owner, not the lender. The less capital invested, the greater the return. For example, if you pay $1,000,000 for a property and sell it one year later for $1,400,000, the return from appreciation is 40%. However, if you had borrowed $500,000 to make the purchase, you would keep $900,000[1] from resale after repaying the loan. This represents an 80%[2] return on the $500,000 invested, less any interest owed on the loan.

There are several caveats associated with appreciation. It should be understood that appreciation is not guaranteed, even in the most secure investment. The real estate owner is subject to the market conditions existing in the local area at the time of resale. If those conditions

---

[1]Resale for $1,400,000 minus $500,000 loan equals $900,000 cash from resale.

[2]Cash from resale equals $900,000 less $500,000 cash invested equals $400,000 profit. Profit divided by cash invested is $400,000 ÷ $500,000 = 80%.

are unfavorable, such as high mortgage interest rates, a declining economy, or an oversupply of comparable properties, market value may actually decline. If you are using leverage, even modest declines in property value may wipe out all of your equity in the property. If the property is producing income or you have enough capital to carry the property, the property may be held until conditions improve. However, such conditions may well depress the overall appreciation realized when the property is eventually sold. In addition, the property will be a very illiquid investment during that period.

For these reasons, a conservative investor does not consider appreciation as the primary source of investment return. For most investments, appreciation should be considered an extra benefit that may or may not materialize. If a project is not attractive unless substantial appreciation occurs, it should be considered speculative.

When analyzing an investment opportunity, it is common to use a projected annual rate of appreciation. In most leveraged investments, the appreciation assumption can significantly affect the attractiveness of the property. If the assumption is too optimistic, virtually any investment can look promising. To guard against this pitfall, you can project a resale value using the same *gross rent multiplier* or *capitalization rate* (*see* INCOME CAPITALIZATION/14) as when purchasing the property. This will mean that the value is expected to increase at the same rate as net operating income. Appreciation will be expected but it will be in line with reasonably expected rental increases.

10

INVESTMENT DRAWBACKS

Although there are significant advantages to investing in real estate, there are serious drawbacks as well. For that reason, real estate may not be the proper investment for many people. However, the disadvantages of real estate investment can also create opportunities for those investors in the position to overcome them. In addition, opportunities are created for middlemen, such as investment *syndicators,* who serve to minimize many of these drawbacks.

One factor that limits the field of real estate investors is the size of the required investment. A down payment on even a modest rental home requires several thousand dollars. Purchasing a sizable commercial property or assembling a diversified portfolio of properties means a much larger investment, certainly beyond the means of the typical investor. Syndicators overcome this problem by gathering a group of investors each of whom purchase shares of a large property or inventory of properties. PARTNERSHIP interests or shares of a *master limited partnership* may be acquired for as little as $1,000. Furthermore, the investor may buy into several partnerships to gain further diversification. Going a step farther, an investor may buy REITs or mutual funds that own real estate. These assets require even smaller minimum investments and are very liquid.

An important consideration in making any investment is its *liquidity,* which is the ease of its convertibility to cash at market value. A highly liquid investment is one that can be converted to cash quickly at market value;

this is a positive attribute. By contrast, an illiquid investment cannot easily be converted to cash. There may be few potential buyers for that type of property at any given time, and none may wish to buy at the time an owner wishes to sell.

Real estate is an *illiquid* investment. This means that, once the investment is made, it is difficult to get your money out quickly, should you need it. It takes at least several weeks, and sometimes months, to sell a property. Market conditions may prevent a sale at a reasonable price. If liquidity is desired, you may purchase shares in a publicly traded syndication, REAL ESTATE INVESTMENT TRUST, or exchange-traded fund (ETF). Many of these are traded on the major stock exchanges and offer immediate conversion to cash.

Because real estate is a physical asset, it requires ongoing management. Purchase of a property is like buying a small business. The owner is responsible for maintaining the property and keeping it producing. Professional property managers or resident managers can be hired to take on many of these responsibilities. The owner still must decide on tenant selection, rental rates, marketing, alterations, and when to sell. However, in a *limited partnership,* the investor can leave these tasks to the general partner.

Until recently, real estate markets were local in nature. There has been a shortage of available information about current prices, rental, and vacancy rates. The typical purchaser is in the market infrequently and cannot stay attuned to current conditions. Therefore, it is difficult to decide on the best offering price for a property or rental rate to charge. Real estate brokers are a good source of such information. Remember, the broker is working for the seller and is under no obligation to advise the buyer on an appropriate price to offer. However, it is possible to hire a broker to find properties for you.

Internet sites have been developed to help make markets more national or global. *Reisreports.com* can provide extensive information on current market status. Also, Costar *(www.costar.com)* is available online to provide data on current lease rents, absorption, and market size in major markets. This is especially useful for property owners, tenants, and prospective builders. Costar also offers information on the sale of individual properties that is particularly useful for appraisers. Property marketing has also gone to the Internet with many brokers putting their offerings online in their web sites. Sites such as *Realtor.com* contain a wealth of information for the residential buyer.

Aside from the size of the investment, the costs of purchasing a property are increased by *transaction expenses*. These include sales commissions, attorney fees, title insurance, appraisal and surveying costs, loan fees, and transfer taxes. A seller may pay as much as 10% of the price of the property in transaction costs. In addition, the buyer may pay 5% or more. These costs tend to make real estate a long-term investment. Short-term profits would have to be substantial to offset transaction costs.

Real estate is *immobile*. For the investor, this means the performance of the property is determined by local market conditions. The demand for the property may be depressed by economic downturn or an oversupply of similar properties. The property cannot be moved to another location where conditions are better. In addition to local market conditions, a property is affected by the quality of the neighborhood and what happens on surrounding properties. Therefore, LOCATION is a major factor in a property's performance. Furthermore, these conditions may change over time. A big part of investment analysis involves evaluating trends in the local market and surrounding area.

What you can do with your property is subject to government policies. On a broad scale, government influence on interest rates and economic trends will affect demand for the property. On a local scale, government can limit your use of the property through ZONING ordinances, building codes, health codes, and environmental laws. In some places a residential project may come under *rent controls*. Decisions to extend streets and utilities can change the attractiveness of your property. For these reasons, real estate investors often take an active interest in the affairs of their local government.

Investors who buy shares of funds traded in public markets find that the value and performance of the assets are affected by more than real estate considerations. Researchers have found that REIT shares act much like small capitalization stocks. So, even though these assets are liquid, an investor may suffer losses if they are sold during a stock market slump.

Drawbacks give rise to opportunities: you may get a chance to buy from an anxious or desperate seller, or to buy in a depressed market. This will occur only if you are bold enough to buy when others are negative about market conditions.

11

RISK

Risk is the chance that things will not turn out as planned. Because no one knows what will occur in the future, risk is an unavoidable fact of life. However, it is possible to anticipate or forecast the future and project a reasonable range of possible outcomes. This is what is meant by the term *calculated risk*. It does not imply that risk can be precisely measured, but that sources of risk can be identified. In this way, it is possible to rank investment opportunities according to their riskiness.

Why would an investor choose to take more risk? Greater risk ought to mean the chance of higher returns. Risk not only introduces the chance that the return will be lower than expected but also that it will be higher. For example, the potential reward from playing the lottery is much higher than the maximum yield from a savings account, but you typically lose your entire "investment" in the lottery, which you won't in the savings account. Because most people are averse to risk, high risk ventures must offer a high potential return to attract investors. Put another way, society often rewards those who are willing and able to take risks. Therefore, to get a high return, you must accept higher risk.

Most people are said to be risk-averse. This means, normally, people prefer less risk to more risk. However, some investors are more sensitive to risk than others. Some are prone to worry about things going wrong and are probably better off with relatively risk-free investments. It should be recognized that no investment is truly risk-free. Real estate rises and falls in value. It is illiquid. Even investing in government-insured bank accounts exposes the investor to the *purchasing power risk* that inflation will wipe out any real return.

Some investors have a greater *capacity* to undertake risk. This capacity depends on the consequences of the investment not working out as planned. If you need CASH FLOW from the investment for the basic necessities of life, you have a low capacity for risk. Any reduction in income would be serious. Likewise, if the invested income is your entire wealth, risk capacity is low. You could weather a reduction in cash flow but would be harmed by loss of capital. An investor with *venture capital,* which is money that he or she is willing to place at risk, can take on more risk. Some investors have what they call "play money," which is not crucial to their financial support, that they can use for speculative ventures. It is important to determine how much risk you are prepared to take and choose investments accordingly.

There are different types of risk. Possibly the most familiar type is **business risk.** This is the chance that the investment will not perform as expected. It may turn out that more capital investment is needed to keep the property going. For example, a major component of the building may fail unexpectedly and need replacing. Or a storm may damage the building. Revenues may drop due to a rise in vacancies or the need to lower rental rates. Operating expenses may increase. Expected appreciation may not be realized when the property is sold. It is even possible that changes in tax laws may affect the return over time. Some of these risks can be reduced by using hazard INSURANCE. Others may be minimized by diversifying investment among different locations and types of property.

A second type of risk is **financial risk.** The chance that you will be unable to make the debt service payments on the property and thus become insolvent. Financial risk is increased by the use of LEVERAGE. The more money borrowed to purchase the property, the higher the chance that a declining net operating income will fail to cover debt service. This is a problem especially if you are poorly capitalized or have most of your capital tied up in illiquid assets. This is why any investment is made more risky by using financial leverage. (Likewise, leverage increases the potential return.) The use of short-term financing also exposes you to *interest rate risk*. This is the chance that interest rates will increase and adversely affect return. Such financing as balloon loans or adjustable rate mortgages presents the possibility that debt service costs will increase if interest rates rise.

Speculation is any situation where you put money at risk depending on some future event. A speculator is hoping for favorable results to occur. If it works out, there will be an especially large reward; if it doesn't, the penalty will be great. This also implies that the hoped-for result is something that the speculator does not control. It may imply that the speculator did not take the time and effort to investigate the situation as would a prudent investor.

For example, you may buy an apartment building with good tenants. You know that if competent management is used, the building will continue to provide income. There is little speculation involved with this investment. On the other hand, a speculator may buy the building with the expectation that it can be converted to commercial use if a new industrial complex is developed nearby. Any expected return from the conversion is speculative because it depends on what happens in the surrounding area.

Speculation often has a bad connotation, sometimes equated to gambling. In addition, some feel that speculation raises costs to the end users in a particular market. For instance, it is believed that housing costs are higher because land speculators increase the prices for development land. Whether that is true or not depends on the circumstances. Speculation has a legitimate purpose. Speculators take on risks that others may not want to accept. For example, speculators often buy farm land in the path of urban development, hoping to sell the land later for a profit. The owner of the land can get a higher price by selling to the speculator and without taking the chance that development will not occur, thereby causing prices to drop. It should be recognized that speculation is a high RISK activity and while the rewards may be large, the chances of failure are great.

In reality, all investments involve some risk. Your return will be affected by things that you can't control. However, the degree of speculation varies depending on the investment and the expectations built into its price. Purchase of a fully occupied building with credit-worthy tenants exposes the owner to the possibility that the local economy will fall apart and rentals will decline. This is a much different situation from a purchase of raw land using a large loan, whereby success of the venture depends on land values soaring before the loan must be repaid.

The key for the successful investor is to recognize the speculative elements of any investment. A smart speculator buys before the market becomes red-hot—when prices are still relatively low. There are times when speculative investing dominates a market, often driving out long-term investors and users. These times are perilous to the investor and may signal the end of a boom.

If you have enjoyed unexpectedly high returns from past investments, you should recognize the role of speculation in those investments. You probably benefited from unforeseen developments that are not likely to recur. Don't make the mistake of thinking you have found the secret to future riches. The proof of an investment strategy is how it performs in bad times, not in good times.

Speculation also refers to building real estate without a tenant or purchaser that is known in advance. In active markets a builder can often make money quickly by building with the expectation of a potential buyer at or near completion, rather than waiting for a buyer who wishes to start from ground level.

12

INVESTMENT
LIFE CYCLE

Like most things, a real estate investment has a beginning and an end. You purchase a property (or share in a partnership) and later sell it, hopefully for a profit. In between, the property may provide income if well managed. This middle period of operation may be long or short, depending on market conditions and the reasons for buying the property. Because of high transaction costs, most investors end up holding real estate for periods of several years.

There are important considerations at each stage of the life cycle of the investment:

Purchase. You will be concerned with getting the right property at a good price and with favorable financing terms. The property should fit your investment objectives. If you want income, you pick a property with proven ability to produce income. If you want appreciation, pick a property with potential for increased value. The price you pay will have a lot to do with appreciation. If you pay above market value, the property will have to improve for you to break even. Financing may determine whether the property makes money or whether you can even keep the property. You must decide how much LEVERAGE to use, knowing that high leverage increases possible returns but may reduce income. Leverage magnifies both potential gains and potential losses.

Operation. During this phase, the property should produce some CASH FLOW. This is the money available to you as an investor. Some properties have negative cash flow, which means you must pay some expenses out of your pocket. A part of cash flow may be due to income tax benefits. Depending on your tax situation, certain tax deductions may allow you to shelter some income from the property from taxes. Remember that cash flow may vary from year to year and depends on your ability to keep enough rent-paying tenants and minimize operating expenses.

Sale. The main benefit from sale is CAPITAL GAIN, the profit on the sale. To make a profitable sale, you will want to maximize the sales price and minimize taxes on the sale. The highest price depends on the timing of the sale. You want to sell when the market is strong. Sometimes, a better price can be had if you are willing to help finance the purchase. To limit your exposure to taxes, you may wish to structure the sale as an *installment sale*. This allows you to spread the income from the sale over several years and may reduce the tax rate on the gain. Also, you may want to arrange an EXCHANGE (see Key 53). If properly done, an exchange can postpone payment of taxes and sometimes avoid payment of taxes altogether.

The key to a successful investment is to consider all of the income expected through the cycle and its timing to determine whether it is worth the cost.

13

INVESTMENT ANALYSIS

Investment analysis is deciding if a particular investment opportunity is right for you. This involves knowing what you want and being able to figure out which investment is likely to satisfy your goals. First, you must determine your investment objectives and translate them into criteria. These criteria allow you to reject inappropriate investments and pick the best of those that are appropriate. Next, you must decide on the type of investment: real estate, stocks, bonds, precious metals. This choice depends on current asset prices and how you expect them to change in the future. It also depends on how your present investment portfolio is composed and how much diversification you need.

After you have some idea of what you want, the next step is to screen the available opportunities to eliminate those that don't fit your criteria. You may seek an expert to help and give instructions of what you would consider. When you have a set of investment alternatives that generally fit your requirements, detailed analysis is used to decide on the best one. This consists of projecting how the investment is likely to perform, considering the chance that something will go wrong, and comparing the projected return to other investment opportunities.

There are several ways to approach the analysis. Some investors like to review all information. Others prefer to play a hunch on what will work. Some like detailed projections. Others base their decision on inspection of the property and surrounding area. Some try to find properties that are undervalued in the market. Others emphasize negotiation to make a profitable deal. Many investors take a short-term perspective and look only at current performance. Others take a long-term viewpoint and look for value appreciation.

Regardless of the approach, a projection of investment return is helpful in making the decision. The return from real estate investments depends on future rent, operating expenses, and financing and tax considerations. By appraising what these will be, you can estimate how the property will perform. Projections may be the main determinant of the decision or may supplement other sources of information. The important thing to remember is that projections are only as good as the assumptions used to make them. In assuming rapid increases in rental rates and unrealistic appreciation rates, any investment can look good. It is best to take a conservative approach to the projection and let speculation about possible improved performance be a separate factor in the decision.

Short-term analysis can be used to screen properties. The following indicators may be calculated quickly with a few bits of information that are based on current performance:

Gross rent multiplier: the price of the property divided by the total gross rent. The lower the number, the less you are paying for the gross income.

Return on investment: the overall rate of return, described below, considers only current cash returns. In order to reflect an expected change in the property value, whether appreciation or depreciation, such is added or subtracted to the numerator. In doing so, the percentage rate will increase with expected appreciation or fall with an expected decline in value. (Depreciation for economic purposes as described here should not be confused with the tax deduction for depreciation, which is just an accounting entry that does not reflect a drop in market value.) However, it is important to understand that current cash flow is more valuable than appreciation. Appreciation in value is an ownership benefit that may be received years later, so it should be discounted to present value. Adding it in full to the numerator is, in effect, mixing apples and oranges, which exaggerates the rate of return.

Overall rate of return or **capitalization rate:** the net operating income (rent less operating expenses) divided by the value of the property. This measure is preferred to the gross rent multiplier because it accounts for operating expenses. Also, it offers a percentage rate, which is a customary way to express rate of return.

Cash-on-cash return or **equity dividend rate:** the cash flow divided by the required equity investment. This is especially useful when you know how the property will be financed. You may use before-tax or after-tax cash flow. If after-tax cash flow is used, you should adjust the returns on alternative types of investment for taxes to make a meaningful comparison.

Return on equity: the cash return on equity may be modified to reflect appreciation or decline in value. Appreciation benefits the equity investor because all of the increase in value accrues to the equity position. Adding appreciation to cash flow can result in a significant increase in the rate of return on equity. However, keep in mind that appreciation is uncertain and is only realized upon a sale, which may not occur for many years. This raises the mixing of investment returns problem. Therefore, expected appreciation should be discounted to present value.

Return of equity: an equity investor receives no return *on* equity unless the full equity investment is or will be recovered, called a return *of* equity. Some investments offer little or no resale value. Whenever the resale amount is less than the original purchase price of an investment, a loss in principal value has occurred. In some cases this is anticipated, as when a coal mine or gold mine is depleted of its ore. A positive return *on* equity does not occur unless the investor recoups—or will recoup—the total amount *of* equity contributed. In any case, however, there is no return on investment unless the investment is, or will be, recovered.

Long-term analysis requires more information and assumptions because you are projecting several years into the future. If you are considering a property whose value is likely to increase or decrease in the near future, or if inflation is significant, long-term analysis is probably worthwhile. The analysis requires that you project growth rates for rents, operating expenses, and property value. Changes in debt service and taxes are also considered. The result of the analysis can be a measure of yield to maturity called the *internal rate of return*. This is the projected annual rate of return over the entire holding period. It can be used to compare other investments with the same holding period. Alternatively, you may calculate the *net present value* of the investment based on your required rate of return. This is often useful when comparing investments that require different levels of cash investment or when putting together a portfolio of several investments. Fortunately, there are computer programs available to do long-term investment analysis. (*See* DISCOUNTED CASH FLOW TECHNIQUES/15.)

14

INCOME CAPITALIZATION

Most real estate investments provide a yearly stream of income. One key investment problem is to figure out how much you should pay for that income stream. If the income is expected to fluctuate from year to year, you may want to use *net present value* (*see* DISCOUNTED CASH FLOW TECHNIQUES/15). But if the income is fairly constant, you can use simple *income capitalization*.

Income capitalization can be used in several situations. You may capitalize net operating income to provide MARKET VALUE of a property. Capitalization of cash flow gives you the value of an investment. In addition, you can find out how much a mortgage loan is worth on the market through capitalization.

To apply this method, you will need two things: a measure of expected income and a capitalization rate. The income measure used depends on the problem. If you are looking for property value, you use *net operating income*. For equity value, use CASH FLOW. For mortgage value, you would use the monthly payments. In each case, the income stream should include a RETURN ON and RETURN OF INVESTMENT.

The form of the capitalization rate also depends on the problem. For property market value, the rate used is called an *overall rate*. These rates may be calculated from market data on recent sales of similar properties. For the investment value application, the rate is called *equity dividend rate*. This rate is the yield you could receive from alternative investments with similar RISK and liquidity. For the mortgage value problem, use the *mortgage constant.* This constant can be found in mortgage tables based on the market rate of interest.

Once the income and rate are found, the capitalization calculation is simple. You divide the income by the rate to get value:

$$\text{Value} = \frac{\text{Income}}{\text{Rate}}$$

Let's work a few examples to illustrate the application of capitalization:

1. A property is projected to provide a net operating income of $15,000 per year. From an appraiser, you find that properties similar to this are selling at an overall rate (net operating income divided by purchase price) of 10%. Therefore, the estimated value of the property is:

$$\frac{\$15,000}{.10} = \$150,000$$

2. You have an opportunity to buy an investment that provides a cash flow after debt service of $3,000 per year. You require a return of 15% to make this equity investment worthwhile, considering the risk of the income declining and what you could get from other investments. Consequently, the most you would pay for the equity investment is:

$$\frac{\$3,000}{.15} = \$20,000$$

The equity is over and above the face value of the mortgages, so the present mortgage balance should be added to derive the property price.

3. You sell a property and take back a note for $40,000 as part of the purchase price. The note

44

calls for monthly payments over 20 years based on interest of 8% per year. You can sell the note in the market, but investors want a yield of 10%. How much can you get for the note?

From a table of mortgage payments, you find the note provides monthly payments of $334.58. A $40,000 loan at 10% for 20 years (remember this is what investors require) would provide payments of $386 per month. You can calculate the mortgage value using a ratio:

$$\frac{\$334.58}{\$386.00} \times \$40,000 = \$34,672$$

This is how much investors would pay for the $40,000 note.

15

DISCOUNTED CASH FLOW TECHNIQUES

Discounted cash flow is a common method for analyzing the expected performance of an investment property. It is more complete than simple one-year measures, such as cash-on-cash return, because it takes into account future years and resale. However, the method depends on assumptions about future growth in rental income and property value. If you are overly optimistic about the future performance of the property, you may be misled by the analysis.

The first step in making a discounted cash flow analysis is to forecast cash flow and resale proceeds. You can start with an operating statement for the most recent year, unless you expect to be able to raise rents or cut expenses immediately or if the property is currently unoccupied (to see how to construct an operating statement, *see* CASH FLOW/5). In most cases, growth rates are selected for rental income, operating expenses, and value. These rates are used to forecast those items of the operating statement. Debt service can be forecast based on the payment schedule for your loan. Income taxes are forecast based on current law.

How far into the future do you make the forecast? Select a period for how long you expect to keep the property. A 10-year period should be sufficient. Then apply the growth rates and make the forecast. (Much of the calculation work can be performed with a computer program. There are a number of commercially available programs designed for the personal computer, or you can create your own program using an Excel spread-sheet.)

The key to discounted cash flow is the discounting process. This process is based on the fact that money expected to be received in the future is worth less than money received today. How much less depends on the *discount rate*. A high rate downgrades future income more than a low rate. The discounting process trans-forms all future expected income into a *present value,* so that you can compare that amount to what you have to invest to buy the property.

There are two basic ways to do discounted cash flow. First, you may select a discount rate and calculate how much you can invest to get a return equal to the rate. This is called *net present value.* Secondly, you may set the amount invested and calculate the discount rate that makes the present value equal to your required invest-ment. This is called *internal rate of return.* Whether you use net present value or internal rate of return depends on how you will negotiate the purchase. If you have a fixed amount to invest, you might want net present value. If you are looking for the highest return, you can use internal rate of return.

While computer programs are available to do the cal-culations, a simple example will give you a feel for how the process works. Consider a property that can be pur-chased for $100,000 with a cash down payment of $10,000. You expect to hold the property for 5 years, after which you think it will sell for $110,000.

To calculate net present value, you select a discount rate of 12%. If you can get a return of 12%, you consider the investment worthwhile. Table 1 shows forecast cash flow, including proceeds from resale after paying off the loan and taxes on CAPITAL GAINS. Also shown are the dis-counted present values of the cash flow using a discount rate of 12%.

The discounted present value is the reverse of com-pound interest. For example, the $893 for year 1 would become $1,000 in a year at 12% interest. Likewise, the $837 for year 2 would become $1,050 in 2 years with interest compounded at 12%. Specifically, $837 would earn $100 interest the first year to become $937, then $937 would earn $113 interest to become $1,050. The same holds for the rest of the computations. So, present value is like applying compound interest, but in reverse.

Table 1

Year	Forecast Cash Flow	Discounted Present Value
1	$ 1,000	$893
2	1,050	837
3	1,100	783
4	1,150	731
5	1,200	681
Resale	20,000	11,349
Present value of cash flow		$15,274

The present value of the cash flow is $15,274. This is greater than the $10,000 needed to purchase the property, indicating that the expected return is more than the 12% required. To get net present value, you subtract the $10,000 from the present value of cash flow. This indicates that you could pay over $5,000 more than the asking price of the property and still get your required return.

If the investment yields more than 12%, how much more? This is where you can use internal rate of return. You can't calculate the return directly, you will need to use trial and error. You keep raising the discount rate until the present value of cash flow equals the required initial investment.

Return to the example and try different discount rates until the present value equals $10,000. In Table 2, we applied discount rates of 15%, 20% and 25%. As you can see, 20% is too low, but 25% is too high. The actual internal rate of return is somewhere in between. You could try rates between 20% and 25% until you got a present value close to $10,000. Again, a computer can run these calculations rapidly and give you a precise estimate.

Because the analysis is so sensitive to your assumptions about growth rates, particularly the resale value, you should use care in selecting these rates. Some investors run several analyses with different assumptions to see how sensitive the return is to future growth. You may want to construct a "worst case" and "best case" to give you a range of possibilities.

Table 2

Year	Forecast Cash Flow	Discounted Present Value		
		15%	20%	25%
1	$ 1,000	$ 870	$ 833	$ 800
2	1,050	794	729	672
3	1,100	723	637	563
4	1,150	658	555	471
5	1,200	597	482	393
Resale	20,000	9,944	8,038	6,554
Present value		$13,586	$11,274	$9,453

There are a number of financial calculators that are pre-programmed to perform these calculations. The most popular and lowest cost are Texas Instruments BA II Plus, BA 35, and Hewlett Packard's 12C. Other calculators may do these and more advanced calculations.

16

MARKET ANALYSIS

A *market analysis* is a study of current supply and demand conditions in a particular area for a specific type of property. Such a study is used to indicate how well a particular piece of real estate will be supported by the market. It identifies the most likely users of the project and how well they are being served by the existing supply of properties. In essence, the study shows if there is a need for a new project, or if an existing project has a good future.

For example, suppose you were considering construction of new luxury apartments in a certain town. A market study would first look at the sources of demand for the units. It would identify a *target market:* the type of tenants most likely to be attracted to the property. This might include their income, typical family structure, and what they desire in a residence. It would then survey the market area to see how many of these people exist and where they live. A good study will project growth trends in the target market, because a likely source of tenants will be new arrivals.

Next, the study will examine supply conditions. The number and location of similar properties is identified. A survey of vacancies indicates how well supply matches demand. Features and characteristics of competing properties should be described and some indication of market rents should be found. In addition, any new projects that will come along should be identified.

Be cautious when investing in an unbalanced market. When the supply of a certain type of real estate is short, rents and prices may be high, but only temporarily. New competition will add to supply and drive prices down. By contrast, when a market is oversupplied with that type of real estate, the price must be low enough to be an attractive investment.

Before determining that a type of land use is in short supply, check public records concerning proposed new development. This information is available from city or county building permit departments, which maintain records on building permits that have been granted or applied for.

Market analysis is a part of FEASIBILITY ANALYSIS. It is used to estimate the pace of rent increase or sales for a new project. This is called the *absorption rate*. It may be expressed as an overall absorption rate—"the market needs 1,000 new apartment units per year"—or a specific rate for the project—"given current competition, the project should capture 200 new rentals per year." This absorption rate estimate is important in projecting the revenue production of a property.

A market analysis may indicate that there is little demand for the type of project envisioned. This would indicate that a change in plans is needed. The project can be redirected to a different target market. The study may also be used to help in the design of the project. It may indicate some feature that is lacking in the existing supply that may give your project a competitive advantage. At the same time, it will probably be necessary to offer the standard features of the competition. The market study will also help in pricing the product for the indicated target market.

Many real estate investors prefer to own the best or highest class of property in the local market (Class A). They feel that if the market becomes overbuilt, they can stay fully occupied by reducing rents. This will draw tenants from Class B and C buildings, whose occupancy and rental rates will drop because of the overbuilt market. Owners of Class B and C buildings will have no similar way to stabilize the falling rental rates or occupancy.

A drop in the value of all property classes, especially B and C, may present opportunities for entrepreneurs. They may be able to buy these buildings at a low price and regain occupancy after performing cosmetic improvements while waiting for a general market recovery from an improved or expanded local economy.

17

SOURCES OF INCOME AND EXPENSE DATA

One of the keys to successful investing is being able to locate reliable, consistent data. Sources of market data for rental income and expense are hereby described.

Nationally Disseminated Rental and Operating Expense Data. Certain national organizations collect information from owners and managers in major cities as to local rents and OPERATING EXPENSES. You can use the information judiciously to determine whether the subject property appears consistent with experience reported nationally. Because the real estate market is fragmented, you must use an appropriate data source for the specific property.

Office Buildings. The Building Owners and Managers Association (BOMA) International provides information on office building rental rates and operating expenses experienced by their members in major U.S. cities. Their address is:

Building Owners and Managers Association
International
1201 New York Ave., Suite 300
Washington, DC 20005
202-408-2662
www.boma.org

Shopping Centers. The Urban Land Institute (ULI) releases a new edition of *Dollars and Cents of Shopping Centers* every three years.

Urban Land Institute
1025 Thomas Jefferson St. NW, Suite 500

Washington, DC 20007
202-624-7000
www.uli.org

Manufactured Housing Communities. Current information on manufactured housing can be obtained from:

Manufactured Housing Institute
2101 Wilson Boulevard, Suite 610
Arlington, VA 22201
703-558-0401
www.manufacturedhousing.org

Apartments, Condos, and Co-ops. The Institute of Real Estate Management (IREM) of the National Association of Realtors periodically provides the *Income/ Expense Analysis* for various types of buildings (elevator, walk-up) in different cities. IREM's address is:

Institute of Real Estate Management
430 North Michigan Ave.
Chicago, IL 60611
800-837-0706
www.irem.org

Hotels and Motels. Sources of information on national and local trends include Smith Travel Research and Pannell Kerr Forster's *Trends in the Hotel Industry*. Addresses are:

STR Global
735 East Main Street
Hendersonville, TN 37075
www.strglobal.com

PKF Texas
5847 San Felipe, Suite 2400
Houston, TX 77057
713-860-1400
www.pkftexas.com

Resort Developments. This organization publishes a monthly review of development news:

American Resort Development Association
1201 15th Street NW, Suite 500
Washington, DC 20005-2842
202-371-6700
www.arda.org

Local Sources of Real Estate Data. Local organizations often collect real estate data, usually for membership use or sale to interested parties. These include the following:

Local Boards of Realtors. Most metropolitan areas have a Board of Realtors, or other broker group, that sponsors a multiple listing service (MLS). Upon the sale of property listed through MLS, the broker must supply information about the completed transaction. Each property sold and its terms of sale are therefore available on computer or in a published book. Some realtor boards provide information to members only; some share with other real estate organizations. Many allow the public to search listings in the MLS over the Internet. In addition, the National Association of Realtors provides a national search at *www.realtor.com*.

Local Tax Assessing Offices. Assessing offices usually keep a file card on every property in the jurisdiction; with property characteristics, value estimate, and estimate derivation. Many jurisdictions are notified of every sale or building permit, for immediate update of affected properties.

Local Credit Bureaus and Tax Map Companies. These may have data on certain parcels; because their main business is not evaluation, they are not a regular source.

University Research Centers. University research centers, many of which are sponsored by broker and salesperson state license fees, may have aggregated data on real estate transactions collected from other sources throughout the state. This data is often helpful in identifying trends established over time and by city for various types of property. Additional research and educational information may be available from such centers. A good site for publications and data, as well as for linkages to other web sites is maintained by the Real Estate Center at Texas A&M University: *recenter.tamu.edu.*

Private Data Sources. Many real estate investors retain files on their property. They will often share information, usually for reciprocity rather than payment.

Property Owner. Property owners' records include permanent records such as deeds, leases, and copies of mortgages (lenders have the original mortgage document) and periodic accounting and tax return information about the property's recent past. An owner's report may be of limited immediate use, however, because it may be disorganized, have extraneous information, or be arranged poorly for appraisals. Also, data from a single property cannot offer a broad perspective on the market.

18

LOCAL ECONOMY

Because real estate can't be moved, its performance depends a great deal on the health of the local economy. A strong, growing economy produces new jobs and needs new office and industrial space. The jobs attract new residents, which in turn means more demand for housing, stores, and recreation. There will be more opportunities to build and higher prices for land suitable for development. Also, vacancy rates will be lower and rents higher for most existing properties.

A local economy that is healthy, but not growing, may still be good for real estate investors. Vacancies will be low, but there are fewer opportunities for builders.

A declining economy means high vacancies and strong competition for tenants. Eventually, many properties will fail and foreclosures will rise. It is difficult to make a property profitable in a down economy. Therefore, you should check out the local economy before buying property.

A local economy may be thought of as having two sectors: *basic* and *service*. The basic sector is the economic specialty of the area and brings money in from outside, like exports are to a country. Basic industry may be manufacturing (Detroit, Pittsburgh), government (Washington), finance (New York), entertainment (Hollywood), or distribution (Atlanta, Dallas, Chicago). The local economy may be highly specialized or may have some of each type. The importance of basic industry is that it often determines the health of the entire economy. This is especially true when the base is concentrated in one industry (oil in Houston) or even one firm (Boeing in Seattle). The smaller the town, the more likely it will be dependent on one industry or firm.

56

The service sector supports local activities. These are the services that residents rely on, such as shopping, gas stations, medical, and business services. The service sector doesn't bring in money from outside but does create a lot of jobs in the economy. The service sector needs and feeds on the basic sector.

Therefore, the key to looking at the local economy is to identify the basic industry and judge its condition. Does the local economy depend on one type of industry or firm? How well is the industry doing and what are its future prospects? Does the economy depend on some natural resource, such as coal mining or agriculture? How well developed is the service sector? There may be investment opportunities if residents have to travel to other towns for basic needs.

Detailed information on local economies can be obtained free of charge from government agencies. The most useful source is the U.S. Bureau of Labor Statistics (*www.bls.gov*). You can download employment data and calculate growth rates to get an idea of how the economy is performing.

You may want to check with the regional Federal Reserve Bank, most of which maintain web sites. In the journals published by these banks, you will find articles on current economic trends.

19

LOCATION AND DEMAND

An old expression in real estate is that the three key aspects of success are "location, location, location." Very similar buildings can have very different values depending on where they are located. In fact, the value of undeveloped land is almost totally determined by where it is.

Location is so important because real estate is more than just space in an economic sense. Its surroundings have a lot to do with how useful the property is. One big reason to buy or rent a piece of property is to be near other activities.

The type of location desired varies with the type of property:

For **residential properties,** people will want to be relatively close to their job and shopping, but not so close that there is a lot of traffic in their neighborhood. Being in a good school district is important to many. The neighborhood should be pleasant and well cared for. A prestige address can add a great deal of value. If the property is apartments, being on a bus route might be important.

Stores and shopping centers need visibility and traffic flow. The property should be near areas where shoppers live or work, depending on the type of stores. Big stores should not be too close to other stores of the same chain. Sometimes proximity to competitors acts like a magnet, attracting customers to the area. In other situations, proximity to too much competition is negative. Small stores tend to be near big stores, hoping to attract shoppers coming and going to the big store.

Office buildings should be close to business activities. Lawyers want and need to be near courthouses or government offices, consultants near corporate headquarters or banks, doctors near hospitals or nursing homes, and other businesses near customers. Because of this need to be close together, downtowns used to be the best place for offices. Today, suburban locations may be just as valuable because of improvements in communications.

Industrial properties should be close to the source of their materials and labor. They have great need for good transportation, with heavy industry often locating on rail lines or near seaports. A good highway is almost a necessity.

In real estate, the best locations get the top dollar. As an investor, you have to look at more than the property alone. Remember, however, that the quality of a location can change over time. Sometimes, a lesser location can become the best place to be. Often, a prime location will deteriorate with economic changes.

Demand. You must always be concerned about the demand for your property. People must want to use the property enough to pay the rents being asked. If the demand to use the property is high, the demand for buying the property will also be high. High demand means top rents, low vacancies, and good resale prospects. Poor demand means rent reductions, high vacancies, and a property that is difficult to sell.

The following are key items that produce demand for real estate:

Economic growth in the local area, particulary job growth, increases demand for all properties. New jobs and residents increase the need for developed real estate. Rising incomes mean better rents and prices, as well as more retail sales (*see* LOCAL ECONOMY/18).

Good quality property raises demand. The property should have all the standard features expected in the market plus something extra that the competition does not have. Appearance, features, size, and services are valued in today's market (*see* MARKET ANALYSIS/16).

A good location improves demand. Location can make a poor quality property profitable while good property can suffer if in the wrong place.

A competitive price can increase demand. If the property is less than ideal, it still may be able to compete on price. It is important to know what segment of the market your project is intended to serve and price it accordingly.

The **cost of alternatives** also determines demand. Apartments are more popular when house prices are unaffordable. Houses sell better when interest rates are low.

The demand for a type of property can be estimated by a market analysis. This will tell you if there is room for more of that type of property in the market. The demand for a specific property is determined by looking at how it compares to other similar properties in features, location, and price.

20

FEASIBILITY ANALYSIS

A *feasibility analysis* looks at how well a particular project is likely to work out for a specific investor. It is a planning tool to decide whether to go ahead with the project or make the investment. These studies are commonly used for new construction or major renovation of a property, particularly when a change in use is intended. In fact, feasibility studies are required for loan applications for proposed projects. Unfortunately, because of this requirement many studies are done after the investor has decided on the project, and are merely papers to satisfy the lender.

A good feasibility study should be a key part of the investment decision and can avoid serious problems after the project has been committed. Pay attention to the analyst's recommendations; use the report to your advantage.

A feasibility study has several major parts. The first section should identify the objectives of the investor. These would include the financial requirements of the investment and what impact the investor wants the project to earn. The analyst needs to nail these objectives down before determining if the project will be successful.

A second part of the study is a thorough MARKET ANALYSIS. This section indicates how the market will accept the project. If the project is completed, how fast will it sell in the market?

A third part surveys the constraints and costs faced by the project. Government regulations that apply to construction, design and operation of the project must be identified. Also included are any private legal constraints, such as deed covenants and easements. The suitability of the site and location for the proposed use is analyzed. Construction and development costs are estimated along with a preliminary development schedule. Finally, financial constraints are detailed. These include projections of financing requirements and cash investment needs during construction and a projection of cash flow through the investor's holding period.

The concluding section of the study presents a projection of projected CASH FLOW and calculation of the return from the project. This is a primary determinant of feasibility and is matched with the stated objectives of the investor. If the project fails to meet the required return of the investor, the project is considered not feasible.

The credentials and qualifications of the analyst should be noted as they will offer clues as to expertise and experience in the type of property under consideration.

Predetermining Financial Feasibility

There are two methods of trying to assure the financial feasibility of a proposed rent-producing investment. One is to determine the operating expenses and debt service that a completed building will incur, setting the rental rate to exceed that sum by a reasonable amount. The other method is to determine the present rental rate in the market. Of course, construction and related building costs must be kept within a strict budget so that market rents will be sufficient to pay for debt service and operating expenses, as well as to provide an adequate return on investment.

Method 1. You can estimate the monthly rental needed by adding debt service payments to anticipated operating expenses. For example, suppose a mortgage loan of $750,000 is required to purchase the land and build a suitable building. Current mortgage terms call for 9% interest with a 10% constant payment. The annual mortgage payment will be $75,000. A 1.25 coverage ratio requires net operating income of at least $93,750. Any operating expenses paid by the landlord (utilities, maintenance, real estate taxes, and such) must be added to achieve the necessary rent. If operating expenses are estimated at $26,250, an annual rent of $120,000 is required. If a 10,000-square-foot building is sought, the rent required is $12 per square foot:

Debt service		_____
times coverage ratio	×	_____
plus operating expenses	+	_____
equals rent required	=	_____
divided by square feet	÷	_____
equals rent required per square foot	=	_____

Conclusion: it is financially feasible at rents equal to or above $12 per square foot.

Debt service		$75,000
times coverage ratio	×	1.25
equals net operating income	=	$93,750
plus operating expenses	+	26,250
equals rent required	=	$120,000
divided by square feet	÷	10,000
equals rent required per square foot	=	<u>12</u>

Method 2. The rent per square foot of leasable area may be fixed by competition in the market. In this situation, you must be assured that costs will be within an allowable budget. For example, suppose the market rental rate is $10.00 per square foot per year, and the landlord is expected to pay $2.00 per square foot for base year taxes and other operating expenses. A building of 10,000-square-feet is planned. Net operating income (NOI) is forecast at $80,000 ($8.00 × 10,000). If the maximum available loan is $666,666, the total cost must be limited to that amount plus any equity you invest.

The net rent of $80,000 ($8.00 per square foot for 10,000 square feet) must be sufficient to pay debt service. If the mortgage carries a 10% annual constant payment, annual debt service is then $66,666, allowing a $13,333 CASH FLOW. Equity investors would pay $111,111 in capital to receive a 12% cash-on-cash return. The total raised from debt and equity sources of capital is $777,777 as follows:

Source	Capital	Annual Requirement
Mortgage	$666,666	$66,666
Equity	111,111	13,333
Total	$777,777	$80,000

Thus, the project is financially viable only if total costs are held under $777,777.

For new construction, total costs include:

- Land
- Land acquisition fees
- Interest during construction
- Construction loan fees
- Permanent loan fees
- Permits
- Building and paving
- Sitework
- Utility hookups
- Legal and accounting
- Builder's and developer's profit

21

MARKET VALUE

Market value, a central concept in real estate, is the amount a property would be expected to bring in a sale when exposed to a competitive market. It serves as a benchmark for a variety of decisions when one considers acquiring and holding a specific property. Although there are other measures of property value, market value is the most commonly used and is the basis for many legal applications, such as condemnation awards, property taxes, and loan underwriting.

Often there is a difference between market value and the worth of a property to an individual buyer. In some cases, you may be willing to accept less than market value because you need cash (or to get out of a burdensome financial obligation) and want a quick sale. The astute investor may acquire such properties at bargain prices. In other cases, you may be willing to pay more than market value (but may not have to) because of a special situation that makes the property especially suitable to you; or you have advance knowledge of news that will greatly improve the property value, such as bringing utilities to a site or widening a street to make it a major artery. Knowing the property's market value may serve as a safeguard against needlessly paying too much for it.

Knowing property value is helpful to the property owner. A period of rising property value may be a good time to sell, rather than waiting until the market has turned and the property is worth less. Market value may provide a benchmark when devising a sales strategy. It is common for sellers to ask more than market value to provide room for negotiation. However, pricing too much above value may discourage buyer interest and create the impression of an undesirable property. Furthermore, a market value APPRAISAL may indicate how the property compares to competing properties.

In essence, market value is the amount of cash that a property would command in a competitive market under ideal conditions. As specified by the appraisal profession, conditions include:

- The buyer and seller are typically motivated (such a transaction is referred to as "arm's length"). Each party is acting in his or her own best interest and is not under pressure to complete the transaction.
- Both parties are well informed or well advised. Each has knowledge of the property and other similar properties on the market.
- A reasonable amount of time is allowed for exposure in the market.
- Payment is made in terms of cash or in terms of financial arrangements comparable thereto. This assures the transaction is a clear-cut sale. For example, a sale may be consummated with the seller accepting a mortgage as part of the sales price. In this case, the true sales price may not be the price stated in the contract because the seller financing may not be at market rates and terms.
- The price represents normal consideration for the property sold unaffected by special or creative financing or sales concessions granted by anyone associated with the sale. Special financing may inflate the price actually paid but represents more than the value of the property alone.

Because of these special conditions, market value may not be an accurate estimate of the price a property may bring under actual market conditions. If that is the object of the value estimate, INVESTMENT VALUE (Key 22) to the highest bidder would be a better value concept to use. To arrive at that amount, the conditions affecting the sale are modified to reflect current market conditions and practices.

Estimate of market value is derived via traditional appraisal—gathering and analyzing market environment data (including local area and immediate neighborhood), considering features and quality of the property and viewing it from several different perspectives to estimate market value.

22

INVESTMENT VALUE

Investment value is what a property is worth to you as an investor. It is the most you can pay and still achieve your investment goals. It may be different than MARKET VALUE, which is the value of the property to the typical buyer in the market. This typical buyer has the usual motivation for buying, an average tax situation, and will use commonly available financing. These factors may not represent your situation. Therefore, your investment value may be higher or lower than market value.

For example, the following situations may make your investment value higher than typical market value:

- The property is ideally suited to your business needs or is located near your business associates.
- You see potential for improvements that are not apparent to the typical investor.
- The seller has an assumable loan but a large amount of cash is needed to close the deal. You have the necessary cash from sale of another property.
- The property offers little tax benefit. You are operating as trustee for a charitable organization and therefore have no need for tax benefits.

If your investment value is higher than market value, you have bargaining room in negotiating for the property. You should be able to get it by outbidding the competition. You should be careful, however, not to go over your investment value.

Investment value to you may be lower than the market value. For example:

- You may be unfamiliar with the area or the type of property.
- The market may be expecting a lot of appreciation that you don't think will happen.
- You don't have a lot of cash and need additional seller financing to make the deal.

If your value is lower than market, you probably won't be a strong bidder for the property. You don't have to offer market value if it is not worth that much to you. You would be better off with no property in that case.

To find out what your investment value is for a particular property, use the techniques of INVESTMENT ANALYSIS. You will want to find the present value of the property assuming your personal situation. A qualified appraiser or real estate investment counselor can do this for you, if so directed.

23

APPRAISALS

An *appraisal* is an expert opinion of value. Appraisals are used in real estate when a professional's opinion of value is needed. Because each property is unique and not traded in a centralized, organized market, value estimates require the collection and analysis of market data.

To understand what appraisals are, you can examine the preceding definition a little more closely. By an expert, we mean someone with the competence and experience to do the type of analysis required. You can get opinions of value from sales agents, the owner, the tenant, or anyone familiar with the property. However, these opinions may not be very useful and probably won't be convincing as evidence of value. Usually, an appraisal expert has attained some type of designation through formal study and examination by a recognized body. For example, the MAI and SRA designations are awarded by the Appraisal Institute to those who pass certain tests, prepare detailed sample reports called demonstrations, and complete years of appraisal experience. At one time, MAI stood for Member of the Appraisal Institute, and SRA stood for Senior Residential Appraiser. Now the letters no longer represent words. The MAI is awarded to those who value commercial, industrial, and apartment properties. The SRA is awarded to those who value residential properties of one to four units. Other organizations that award appraisal designations include the National Society of Real Estate Appraisers, the American Society of Appraisers, the International Association of Independent Fee Appraisers, and the National Association of Master Appraisers. Designations from legitimate associations assure that the appraiser understands the principles of appraisal and subscribes to a code of professional ethics. State certified or licensed appraisals are required for most or all transactions in each state.

An *opinion* is a judgment supported by facts and logical analysis. The appraiser considers all available information that reflects on the value of the property. He or she follows a logical process to arrive at the opinion. The result is not merely a guess but a careful reading of the facts in the case. A good appraiser avoids interjecting personal bias into the opinion but tries to figure out how the market views the property.

Value should be qualified as well. There are different types of value. The majority of appraisals seek to find MARKET VALUE (see Key 21). This is what the property is worth to typical purchasers in a normal market. It is used as a standard in many applications. If you are interested in what the property is worth under your personal circumstances, an appraisal can be made for INVESTMENT VALUE (see Key 22). An appraiser should be able to give an opinion of value under various conditions—as long as they are made clear at the outset.

Appraisals are typically written in certain formats. Most residential property appraisals are prepared on a preprinted form that has universal recognition and acceptance. It is called the Uniform Residential Appraisal Report (URAR). It is used for single-family appraisals and housing with up to four dwelling units.

Commercial property reports are generally narrative—that is, written in standard paragraph form—and include tables and charts. Three reporting formats are available: Self-Contained, Summary, and Restricted. The Self-Contained Report includes a great deal of detail and is costly and time-consuming to prepare. A Summary Report has less written detail and is probably the most commonly used. A Restricted Report is shorter. It is so abbreviated that its use is restricted to the party who ordered it because its brevity may prevent others from understanding it. Summary appraisals are the most frequently used written format.

The extent of research provided by an appraisal may be described in a section called the *scope*. The scope of work should be determined by the appraiser as being adequate to solve the problem and comparable to what the appraiser's peers would do to provide a credible appraisal. If an appraisal is not credible, the appraiser has violated the Uniform Standards of Professional Appraisal Practice (USPAP).

Most appraisals are used for factual support. Lenders use them to show that a property is worth enough to serve as collateral for a loan. They may be used in condemnation cases to award compensation. They can be used to challenge property tax assessments or to back up a deduction on an income tax return. They may be used in settling an estate.

Appraisals may be used as decision tools as well. They may help in offering a property for sale or making an offer to buy. They may serve to assist banks when trying to manage repossessed properties or to work out a troubled project.

An appraisal report contains several standard sections that describe the process followed by the appraiser to get to the value opinion. There should be an opening section that describes the intent of the report: what type of value and any conditions applied, including the date when the value opinion is valid. This is followed by several sections describing the property and conditions in the market and area around the property. Often there is an analysis showing the *highest and best* use of the property. This is most important when there is some potential for an improvement in use of the property. The next sections show how different indications of value are derived. There are three basic ways to get a value indication: sales comparison, income analysis, and replacement cost approaches. Each one should be explained with the data used and how it was analyzed. The reconciliation section of the report shows how a final opinion was arrived at from all the information and analysis described previously.

24

LEVERAGE

Most real estate investments are made with some borrowed money. Real estate is expensive, so few investors have enough cash to buy a property without using a loan. Even if you had the cash, you probably wouldn't want to tie up so much of your investment budget in one property. Most interest is tax deductible, and financing gives you the added benefit of diversification in your investment program.

When you use borrowed money, you have financial leverage working for you. Leverage tends to magnify investment return—you are controlling a relatively large property with a relatively small cash investment. You get to keep any income from the property after you make the loan payments. That income can be substantial when compared to the amount of cash you have invested. However, leverage also increases the RISK of your investment. There is a greater chance that there will be no income left after you pay all expenses.

To see how leverage works, consider the following examples. Suppose you bought a building for $1,000,000 cash that produces a net operating income of $120,000 per year. Your annual income is the $120,000, giving you an annual return of 12%. If you had used a loan of $800,000 to buy the property, your cash investment would have been only $200,000. For simplicity, suppose the loan called for interest-only annual payments of $80,000 (10% interest). Your CASH FLOW would be the $40,000 left over after you paid the lender. Leverage increases your return on equity to 20% ($40,000 divided by $200,000).

Leverage worked to your benefit in this case because the interest rate of the loan was lower than the rate of return from the property. Suppose the loan had required payments based on an interest rate of 15% ($12,000 per year). The loan payments would take up the entire net operating income from the property and you would be left with no cash flow (your return would be zero). This *negative leverage* resulted from the loan being too costly compared to the property's return.

Because leverage increases risk, the amount of borrowed money used should be limited. Suppose in our example, you discovered that a lender is willing to lend you $950,000 at 10% interest to buy the property. You calculate that your cash flow would be $25,000, but your cash investment is only $50,000. This provides a return of 50% a year. What would happen if you have to reduce rents and end up with a net operating income of $90,000? You would have a negative cash flow of $5,000[1] and a negative return on your investment.

Leverage also works on the profits from resale. Suppose you buy a piece of land for $1,000,000 and sell it one year later for $1,150,000. Your return is 15%. You might have borrowed $800,000 to make the purchase, requiring a $200,000 cash investment for equity. After paying back the loan with 10% interest, you have $270,000 left from the sale. Your return is now 35% ($70,000 profit on a $200,000 cash investment).

As before, the investment has been made more risky by the use of leverage. Suppose the property had sold for only $1,050,000. The all-cash deal would have provided a positive return of 5%. However, using the loan would push your return negative, because you would have only $170,000 left after paying back the loan with interest. At very high levels of leverage, any decline in value may completely wipe out any equity you have in the property.

---

[1]$90,000 net operating income minus $95,000 debt service equals $5,000 negative cash flow.

25

MORTGAGES TO FINANCE REAL ESTATE

Mortgage loans are used to finance most real estate purchases. These loans are a form of secured financing. When you get a mortgage loan, you are actually signing two documents. The first is a *note,* by which you give your personal pledge to repay the loan on time, as agreed in the loan contract. The second is a *mortgage* or *deed of trust,* which gives the lender an interest in the property to back up your pledge. If you fail to make timely payments, the lender can *foreclose* on the mortgage and take the property to satisfy the debt. The property will be sold and proceeds will be applied to the unpaid loan. If any is leftover, the borrower is entitled to it. If proceeds are less than the debt, the lender may sue for a *deficiency judgment.* This means the lender can claim cash or other property from you to make up the deficit.

A property that has no liens is said to be *free and clear.* A mortgage creates a *lien* on the property, which gives the lender the right to foreclose. The lender can require that you insure the property, pay property taxes on time, and maintain the upkeep of the property. In many cases, the lender will require that you pay into an *escrow* account for payment of insurance premiums and tax assessments.

A property may have more than one mortgage. For example, a $1,000,000 property may have a first mortgage for $800,000 and a second mortgage for $100,000. The second mortgage may have been put on at the time of purchase to help finance the down payment or later to take equity out of the property (*see* REFINANCING/31). The interest rate and other conditions of a second mortgage loan may be less favorable than the first because the second lender is not as well covered against default. By buying a property with a low down payment, such as with a mortgagee insured by the FHA, you may avoid the need for a second mortgage.

Sometimes it is possible for an investor to arrange a *nonrecourse* mortgage loan on the property. This forces the lender to look only to the property for satisfaction of debt in case of a default. The liability of the borrower is then limited to what he or she has invested in the property (*see* LIMITING LIABILITY ON MORTGAGE DEBT/30).

Most mortgage loans are *amortizing:* some of the loan payment is used to repay the principal borrowed. With a level-payment loan, all payments are the same. The portion going to pay interest gradually falls and the remainder is devoted to principal. Early payments are mostly interest and the last payments are mostly principal.

Many loans have *due on sale clauses:* the loan must be repaid if the property is sold. It is often an advantage to have a loan that can be assumed by a buyer of the property. This makes it easier for the buyer to arrange financing. If interest rates have risen, an assumable loan can add to the price you get for the property because the buyer will enjoy lower loan payments. Loans with FHA insurance generally are assumable.

Another important feature of a mortgage loan is the *prepayment privilege.* Some loans require payment of a penalty if the loan is paid back early. This increases the cost of refinancing or of retiring the loan at resale. You should try to get a loan that does not require a penalty for early retirement (*see* FINANCING TERMS/29).

A *deed of trust,* which is used instead of a traditional mortgage in many states, is similar to a mortgage but may facilitate the foreclosure process. Property ownership is held by an independent third party, the trustee, who acts after a default occurs. The borrower may then bring the payments current, but if he or she doesn't, the trustee may be ordered by the court to turn the title over to the lender.

26

GETTING A LOAN

When you apply for a MORTGAGE loan, the lender will be concerned with two things: do you have the ability to make loan payments and is the property worth enough to support the loan? This determines how much RISK is taken on by the lender making the loan.

The process of figuring out how risky a loan would be is called *underwriting*. Most lenders have requirements or standards they apply when underwriting a loan. Often these requirements are set by companies that buy loans from the original lender. Whether a lender sells the loan or keeps it, that lender tries to conform the loan to these standards so it could be sold if necessary.

If the loan application fails to meet the standards, the lender may deny the loan. Alternatively, the loan may be made, but for a lesser amount or at a higher interest rate. In some cases, the lender may require more collateral to make the loan you want.

When underwriting, the lender will check your credit record to see if you are a good risk. In addition, the lender will look at the property to see if it can support the loan. An APPRAISAL will be made. A *loan-to-value ratio* is calculated by dividing the amount of the loan by the appraised value. The lender knows that if you have some of your own money tied up in the property, you are more likely to keep making payments. Also, if the loan must be foreclosed, the property should be worth enough to repay the loan balance. Generally, loans on owner-occupied homes are made for no more than 80% of value (higher if mortgage insurance is used). Income-property loans may require a lower loan-to-value ratio, typically 75%.

Another measure of risk used in underwriting compares income to debt payments. For home buyers, lenders use the ratio of personal income to monthly payments. For income property, the *debt coverage ratio* (net operating income divided by debt payments for a year) is used. Lenders usually like to see net operating income at least 20% higher than debt service (a minimum debt coverage ratio of 1.20). When commercial tenants have high credit ratings and sign a long-term lease, a low ratio might be accepted. By contrast, when leases are short or with transient tenants, a higher ratio is required. If the loan-to-value ratio is too high or debt coverage is too low, a reduction in the loan amount will make the loan less risky for the lender. This may allow you to qualify for the loan.

27

MORTGAGE SOURCES FOR INVESTMENT PROPERTY

Knowing where to find money to finance a real estate purchase is one of the keys to successful real estate investment. Financial institutions that are important to individuals who want to borrow on real estate are:

Life Insurance Companies. Large life insurance companies are usually interested only in loans that exceed $1 million. They lack the facilities to service many small loans and therefore prefer a smaller number of large loans. With billions of dollars in assets, some life insurance companies can make very large loans—$10 million or more in some cases. Life insurance companies rarely offer construction loans; they are conservative and want the long-term yield and safety provided by permanent mortgages on finished products.

Commercial Banks. Commercial banks are active in making construction loans on all types of property. Such loans are usually offered only if the borrower has a *take-out commitment* from a permanent lender; upon project completion, the permanent loan will "take" the bank "out of" (repay) the construction loan.

Savings and Loan Associations and Mutual Savings Banks. Savings and loan associations (S&Ls) and mutual savings banks (MSBs) primarily offer residential first mortgages on local property, including one-to-four-family houses. Only the largest S&Ls offer loans of more than $1 million on a single project, although many are willing lenders on multi-family properties in the

$100,000–$1,000,000 range. Many S&Ls and MSBs offer construction loans to builders; for a *commitment fee,* some will also offer the privilege of permanent financing at a predetermined interest rate.

Mortgage Bankers and Brokers. These companies make loans on behalf of other investors, which bankers then service for a fee. They will originate any type of loan they can sell. Because they deal with borrowers and lenders in the same transaction, mortgage bankers and brokers must know both sides of the market for commercial property loans.

Real Estate Investment Trusts. Real estate investment trusts (REITs) invest in construction loans, permanent mortgage loans, equities, and leasing arrangements. Each REIT may specialize in just one or two of these types of investments.

Pension Funds. Pension funds often acquire permanent mortgages on income-producing properties. In recent years, many also have bought equities in large income-producing properties, or have acquired properties without the aid of mortgage financing.

Credit Unions. These organizations have become active in the residential real estate mortgage market.

28

TYPES OF LOANS

Various types of loans are used to finance real estate. The variety comes from differences in how interest is charged, the term of the loan, and any extra rights provided to the lender.

Adjustable-rate mortgages (ARMs) provide an opportunity to enter an investment at a lower initial interest rate, but with the risk that the rate may rise later on. The first-year rate is usually indexed (tied to) a short-term rate such as the Prime rate or the one-year U.S. Treasury Bill rate. This rate is adjusted periodically, usually each year, with a "cap" on both the annual amount of increase and a "lifetime rate cap" over the life of the loan. For example, an ARM might start out at 5% and be adjusted once a year with the annual rate increase limited to two percentage points, not to exceed six percentage points over the life of the loan. If all adjustments resulted in increases of two percentage points, the interest rates over seven years would look like this:

Year	Interest Rate
1	5%
2	7%
3	9%
4	11%
5, 6, 7 . . .	11%

Of course, the rate rises only if the rate indicated by the index goes up. Rates may also go down. The ARM protects the lender from rising rates, and it offers lower entry-level rates (payments) to the investor. For borrowers, the adjustable-rate mortgage (ARM) is riskier than a fixed-rate loan because large index rate increases can increase monthly payments significantly. When interest rates fall, however, the borrower's periodic payment is reduced. Typically, ARM contract interest rates are initially one to two percentage points below interest rates on fixed-rate loans.

A **permanent loan** is underwritten for 15 to 30 years. It is often fully amortized (that is, principal is repaid through monthly payments) over the loan term.

Balloon loans and **miniperm loans,** also called "bullet" loans, have terms from three to twenty years; generally, the longer the term, the higher the rate. The balance must be paid in a lump sum at the end of the loan term; this balance is called a "balloon payment" or *bullet*. Miniperms are usually offered by the construction lender to pay off the construction loan and provide time for the borrower to obtain permanent financing. Miniperm loan terms are usually two to seven years. Interest rates are high compared to long-term rates (about two percentage points above the Prime rate) and usually are readjusted each time the Prime rate changes. The amortization schedule is long-term (possibly 30 years); but a balloon payment comes due long before the loan can be fully amortized. Miniperms entail more risk to the borrower compared with long-term fully amortized loans. A *bridge loan*, to bridge the gap between the construction loan and the permanent loan, is a type of miniperm.

Participation mortgages, often referred to as *equity participations,* provide an inflation hedge to the lender. The borrower gives up rights to a portion of annual earnings. The expectation is that inflation will increase the property's income. Payments are based on an annual debt service (ADS) payment plus a percentage of gross income (or net operating income, NOI) above a specified level. (Lenders prefer to use gross income because amounts are easier to validate by audit.) Assume a $1 million fixed-rate loan at an interest rate of 9% for 26 years. The ADS payment is $100,000. Gross income is $300,000. The participation might require an additional payment of 10% of gross income in excess of $250,000 per year: $300,000 less $250,000 is $50,000; 10% of $50,000 is $5,000. Therefore, $5,000 is the additional mortgage payment required for participation.

Interest-only loans are used to minimize debt service and maximize tax benefits (mortgage interest can be fully deducted as an expense whereas principal reduction is not tax-deductible). The borrower makes a periodic payment equal to the interest accrued on the original principal amount. The interest-only period may be for a portion of the life of the loan (after which the loan begins to amortize) or for the entire loan term. There are loans in which the borrower is required to pay the interest only. The principal amount is paid in full at the end of the loan term.

29

FINANCING TERMS

Arranging the best financing can be as important as negotiating the best price for a property. Before you talk to a lender, however, you should understand how the various terms of a loan can affect your investment.

Interest Rate. Interest is a charge for the use of money. The lower the rate, the more attractive the loan. The degree of LEVERAGE is also important. Many investors will pay a significantly higher interest rate in order to enjoy a lower cash down payment and therefore be able to exercise more leverage. Some equity investors will pay higher prices for property to achieve more leverage. Sellers sometimes accommodate by providing financing to buyers or by paying *discount points* on a buyer's loan, but they will try to raise their price to compensate. Consequently, prices are generally increased by favorable financing.

Degree of Leverage. When interest rates are low, the loan amount is usually limited by the *loan-to-value* (L/V) ratio (*see* GETTING A LOAN/26). When rates are high, the *debt coverage ratio* (DCR) usually sets the maximum loan amount. For conservative lenders, the L/V ratio is usually in the range of 65% to 70%. Other lenders may use a L/V ratio criteria of 75% to 80%. A conservative DCR is around 1.25.

Amortization Term. The longer the amortization term of a mortgage loan, the lower the annual debt service, and therefore the greater the annual CASH FLOW. However, once loan terms are stretched beyond 30 years, the annual mortgage payment requirement declines, but the change is quite small. Annual debt service can never become less than the interest due on the principal balance. Many loans on income property become due years before being fully amortized. These are called *balloon payment* loans (*see* TYPES OF LOANS/28).

Prepayment privileges allow the borrower the right to pay off the remaining debt before it is due. Some loans include penalties for prepayment, although usually the penalty declines with time. For example, the penalty may be 3% if the loan is prepaid during the first five years, 2% the next five years, then declining by 0.5% for each of the following years until there is no penalty. Some mortgage loans are locked in for the first five to ten years; prepayment without the lender's consent is prohibited.

Exculpation is freedom from liability. When a mortgage loan includes an exculpatory clause, the property is the sole collateral for the loan. Should the property be foreclosed, the lender can look only to the property for full satisfaction of the debt, not to other property you own. In the absence of exculpation, you usually are personally liable for the debt. *Nonrecourse* is another term used to describe mortgages with exculpatory clauses; the lender's only recourse in the event of borrower default is to the property itself, not to your personal assets.

Assumability is the borrower's right to transfer the mortgage loan with the property to another party. Because the new owner may not be as good a credit risk as the original owner, lenders often reserve the right to approve a loan assumption. In recent years, some lenders have been willing to approve changes routinely, provided that they can *escalate* (increase) the interest rate on the debt. Such provisions in mortgage loans make assumption privileges less attractive. Despite lender approval of changes in assumption, original borrowers remain liable for the mortgage debt. So if there is a default on an assumed loan, sellers are liable, but they can try to collect from their buyer. By contrast, if the buyer took the property "subject to" the loan, but did not assume it, the sellers remain solely liable for default.

A *novation* may be used to free the seller from future liability of an assumed mortgage. A novation is a three-party agreement that releases one party (the original borrower) from an agreement and substitutes a new party (the new property owner, who assumes the loan). However, all parties (buyer, seller, lender) must agree to the novation.

Call or acceleration provisions are effectively balloon payment provisions. Although the loan has a 25- or 30-year term, lenders, at their option, can accelerate payment of the principal after 10 or 15 years, regardless of whether the loan is in default. This obviously puts the lender in a strong position. Upon reaching the "call" date, the lender can force repayment or escalate the interest rate.

Subordination means moving a mortgage loan to a lower priority. The priority of a lender's claim is where the lender stands in line for collection after a foreclosure. Land financed by a seller with a first mortgage and now ready for development is not acceptable collateral for a construction lender. Construction lenders want a first lien. If the holder of an existing mortgage is willing to subordinate, the existing mortgage will be reduced to a second lien position to allow a first lien for the new mortgage. If a subordination clause will be needed, you should attempt to insert it initially; lenders are reluctant to reduce collateral later. Subordinated loans are more favorable to borrowers because they increase the flexibility of first-mortgage financing.

30

LIMITING LIABILITY ON MORTGAGE DEBT

When you take out mortgage financing, you should seek ways to limit the extent of a loss to the smallest amount possible. *Exculpation* means freedom from liability. With exculpation, the property is the sole collateral for the loan. The loan is called *nonrecourse* because the lender can look only to the mortgaged property to satisfy the debt. The lender has no recourse to any other property or income of the borrower.

When you finance property you should try to make it the sole collateral for the debt. If it is not, and the property declines far enough in value, you could lose not only all of the money you invested as equity but anything else you own may have to be sold to pay for the subject property debt. Even with a foreclosure, the lender may claim not only the property but also a *deficiency* between the property's value at foreclosure and the amount owed. From the start, you may include an *exculpatory clause* in the mortgage document. This often may be arranged when the seller is providing a loan, and is able to negotiate on an equal footing with a lending institution. However, for construction loans and small residential properties, institutional lenders are reluctant to grant such a provision.

Another way to limit liability is for the investor to form a shell or nominee corporation which buys the property and borrows against it. A newly formed corporation or one with no assets may be used. Immediately after the acquisition, the corporation transfers the assets to the true owner who takes it subject to the mortgage but does not assume the mortgage. Alternatively, a corporation, LIMITED LIABILITY COMPANY, or LIMITED PARTNERSHIP may be formed to buy, borrow, and operate the property (see Key 40). However, each form may have tax or other financial characteristics that are not entirely desirable. An attorney and CPA must be consulted.

While some lenders will cooperate with property buyers to limit liability to facilitate the sale or financing, others will insist on personal guarantees. But it is prudent to try to limit exposure to losses in every legal way possible.

31

REFINANCING

At some point during the ownership of a real estate investment, it may be worthwhile to refinance a property. This involves replacing the existing financing with a new loan. Refinancing is used to reduce debt service or to take equity out of a property. Cash from refinancing may be used for other purposes or to help finance another investment.

Refinancing can be expensive. Taking out a new loan requires payment of origination fees, application fees, and discount points. Retiring the old loan may require payment of a prepayment penalty. In some cases, when you refinance with the same lender that made the original loan, some of the costs are waived. This depends on whether the lender wants to keep the loan. The biggest cost is often discount points on the new loan. Each point is a one-time charge equal to 1% of the loan. You can reduce these costs by finding a loan with no or few points. Also, some lenders will finance the costs with the new loan, reducing the cash you need to refinance.

Refinancing can be used to reduce the cost of debt service when interest rates have declined. The new loan is made for the amount of the old loan balance, but with a lower interest rate. The savings in payments must be enough to outweigh the costs of the refinancing. You can calculate the number of months it takes to pay back the costs by dividing the total costs of refinancing by the monthly difference in payments.

You can cash in some of your equity when the value of the property has risen. This is done by refinancing for an amount greater than the old loan.

Another use of refinancing is to improve the terms on the debt. The existing loan may have a balloon payment due in a few years or it may be an adjustable-rate loan. When long-term, fixed-rate loans are available at reasonable rates, it may be prudent to change over before you are forced to seek new financing.

Unless the market has been strong since you bought the property, you may want to get an appraisal before applying for financing. If the market value of the property has fallen, you may be unable to refinance for the amount you owe. For example, a property was purchased five years ago for $100,000 and now has an outstanding loan debt of $90,000. Unfortunately, when the bank appraises the property, it finds the current value has fallen to $85,000 and is willing to fund only $80,000 on the new loan. You would have to come up with $10,000 in cash investment to accomplish the refinancing. Therefore, in times when property values are falling, some owners find they cannot raise the cash to take advantage of lower interest rates to reduce their debt service.

32

GROSS INCOME

Potential gross income is the rent collectible if all units are fully occupied. In estimating potential gross income, you should distinguish between *market rent* (economic rent) and *contract rent*. Market rent is the rate prevailing in the market for comparable properties. Contract rent is the actual amount agreed to by landlord and tenant.

The key to successful investing often is identifying situations in which the contract rent can be sharply increased to the market rent in the near future. Various rental units of comparison can be used to determine whether the contract rent is below market.

Potential gross income is also called *gross scheduled income* or *gross rent possible*. It is the full amount of rent if all units are occupied all year.

In the majority of office building and shopping center leases, there are additional charges for *common area maintenance* (CAM). The costs of maintaining the common areas—hallways, lobbies—are billed to the tenants in proportion to the square footage they occupy. Tenant reimbursements for the expenses—utilities, cleaning, and taxes—are typically included as potential gross income.

Rental Units of Comparison. Rents must be compared in terms of a common denominator. Typical units of comparison are square-foot, room, apartment, space, and percentage of gross business income of the tenant.

When the square-foot unit is used with an office building or shopping center, you should note that some leases are based on *gross leasable area* (GLA) and others on *net leasable area* (NLA). NLA is the floor area occupied by the tenant. GLA includes NLA plus common areas such as halls, restrooms, and vestibules. An office building with 100,000 square feet of GLA might have only 80,000 square feet of NLA, a difference of 20%. When leases are compared, it must be known whether rent is based on GLA or NLA.

Other rental units of comparison are rent per month and rent per year. Local custom and type of property will determine whether rent is stated per month or per year. Rent per month must not be compared with rent per year.

Vacancy and Collection Allowance. The lost income expected from vacancies and bad debts must be subtracted from potential gross income. The lost income is calculated at the rate expected of local ownership and management. If a property is especially well or poorly managed, rates differ from the average, which is attributable to management, not the property.

Special problems occur in analyzing properties occupied by a single tenant. You must evaluate creditworthiness and length of lease term, then estimate probability of a vacancy in the future and when it might occur.

Miscellaneous Income. Miscellaneous income is received from concessions, laundry rooms, parking space or storage bin rentals, and other associated services integral to operating the project. It includes any money reasonably related to the ordinary operation of the project, but not money earned from individual entrepreneurial activities of the owner or property manager.

Effective Gross Income. Effective gross income is the amount remaining after the vacancy rate and bad debt allowances are subtracted from potential gross income and miscellaneous income is added. Calculating effective gross income is an intermediate step in deriving CASH FLOW.

33

LEASE PROVISIONS

A *lease* is a legal document that provides the key to a successful relationship between the owner and tenant. Negotiations between the owner and tenant concern the type of lease used and the nature of the lease clauses included. Whereas anything legal may be written into a lease, a description of common lease provisions for commercial tenants follows. (*Also see* LEASE RENT/34 and PERCENTAGE LEASES/35.)

Date and Parties. The lease states the date the lease agreement is reached, when the lease is valid, and the names and addresses of the parties. The lessor is typically referred to as the "landlord"; the lessee is the "tenant."

Premises is the property being leased. It consists of land, buildings, and other improvements that exist or will be built. Many leases require an exhibit or supporting schedule to describe the premises in sufficient detail, including land boundaries, to avoid a misunderstanding about the property.

Term. The duration of a lease is crucial in the arrangement with a tenant. For commercial property that must be financed, permanent lenders look to the length and strength of the lease. While the term of a lease and that of permanent debt need not coincide, having the two reasonably close to each other facilitates financing. If the lease is short-term, expect a lower loan-to-value ratio from a lender.

Alterations. A typical alteration clause in a lease requires the tenant to obtain the landlord's permission and approval of the plans. The tenant must maintain insurance for the work and hold the landlord harmless for any claims or liens arising from construction.

Insurance. In a long-term commercial lease, the tenant is typically expected to provide insurance to protect the landlord from all claims throughout the lease term, including liability and hazard insurance; furthermore, the tenant is required to show the landlord policies bearing at least the minimum amount of insurance required by the lease. In a short-term lease on a single-family house or duplex, the landlord is expected to carry liability insurance and hazard insurance on the structure (though not on the contents).

Taking. Commercial leases typically provide for termination of the lease if a substantial portion of the building is taken by the government under *eminent domain,* or if some portion (20% or more) of the parking is taken, unless the landlord substitutes a nearby parking area. In the event of lease termination caused by eminent domain, the lease should state that the tenant has no claim against the landlord. The tenant may have a claim against the condemnor for lost business.

Assignment, sublease is transfer by the tenant to someone else of all his/her lease rights in the property. *Subletting* occurs when the tenant retains some of the property or at least some rights and negotiates a separate lease with the "subtenant." As a landlord, be sure your lease requires your approval of assignment or subletting as that is the only prudent course of action. In addition, neither procedure should release the original tenant from the lease.

Subordination. The earliest documents recorded at the courthouse have the highest priority. As early documents are released, such as a mortgage that is paid off, those next in line move up to the highest priority. There must be a subordination clause in a lease so that the property owner can secure a first mortgage without the lease having priority. However, to protect the tenant, the lease should state that tenant rights should not be affected by any mortgage unless the tenant is in default under the lease.

Fixtures. Typically, commercial leases allow tenants to install their own fixtures, but protect a landlord by requiring the fixtures to be approved by the landlord in advance, to be good quality products, and to be removed at the end of the lease term with the property restored to its original condition except for normal wear and tear.

Destruction. A lease should provide for the event of total or partial destruction of the property by fire or other accident. In the event of total destruction, either party should be allowed to terminate the lease. If property is partially destroyed, the landlord should be allowed to rebuild unless the damage is extensive or the remaining term of the lease is brief. Rent abatement during reconstruction is a negotiated item.

Default. Possible types of tenant default must be listed in the lease. You should terminate the tenant's right to possession upon any default. Examples of tenant default include being late in rent, becoming bankrupt or insolvent, or vacating the premises.

Surrender. Upon termination of the lease, the tenant should return the property in good condition, allowing for normal wear and tear or damage resulting from the landlord's neglect or negligence. The property should be free of any liens the tenant caused and of all subleases created by the tenant. Generally, fixtures that have become part of the realty remain, while *trade fixtures*—those needed to operate a specific business—are to be removed.

Arbitration. Some leases call for binding arbitration to settle disputes, which usually is easier or less costly than litigation. Some name a specific arbitration board to resolve disputes. Mediation or conciliation (nonbinding) may also be used to resolve disputes.

Various other provisions frequently used in a commercial lease include:

Waiver: When either party does not strictly require lease performance, that party's rights are not waived.

Encumbrances: The property is delivered to the tenant without liens except those agreed upon in advance.

Quiet Enjoyment: This covenant promises that the landlord will not interfere with a tenant who abides by the lease.

Signs and Awnings: Allows a tenant to install signs with the landlord's advance approval.

Brokers: Specifies the brokerage firm for the lease and commissions payable.

Notices: Requires notices to be sent, typically by registered mail, with return receipt, using the last known address.

Estoppels: Requires tenant to provide a certificate stating that the tenant is properly occupying and using the property and is not in default, and requires tenant to certify other reasonable requests.

While you can't expect a prepackaged form to be perfectly suitable for all applications, you can get a start on creating a functioning lease with the help of online suppliers of forms. Examples include

- *MrLandlord.com*
- *Agreementsetc.com*
- *exlandlordforms.com*
- *Findlegalforms.com*

Be sure to check the lease thoroughly to see if it meets your purposes before adopting it as a working lease.

34

LEASE RENT

A *gross* lease is one where the landlord pays all of the operating expenses: utilities, property taxes, insurance, and repairs. A *net* lease is one where the tenant pays all of those expenses. In practice, most leases are hybrids where certain expenses are paid by the landlord and others by the tenant, which causes new terms to be coined, such as "triple-net," to describe a lease where the tenant pays all expenses.

Long-term leases of single-tenant buildings tend to be net. The tenant can control and incur expenses to suit itself. The tenant should be required to prove it has paid tax assessments and insurance. Short-term leases of multi-tenant buildings, such as apartments, are usually gross. Common management and maintenance of the building serves the tenants better than if each were to arrange its own repairs and maintenance.

A typical lease requires *base rent* paid each month at the beginning of the month. Especially with a long-term lease there may also be additional rent based on change in the Consumer Price Index (CPI), tenant sales, operating expense or tax stops, and maintenance costs. PERCENTAGE LEASES are required of retail tenants in some properties.

Leases for multiple years without rent adjustments for inflation may impose hardships, usually on landlords. In recognition of a lengthy lease term, a cost-of-living adjustment may provide for additional rent based on some published index.

The index, frequency of adjustment, and amount of adjustment are negotiable. The Consumer Price Index, published by the Bureau of Labor Statistics of the

U.S. Department of Labor, is typically used as a basis for adjustment because of its frequency of computation and widespread publication. A lesser-known local index tied to rental rates, operating expenses, or real estate values may be satisfactory but may introduce an element of instability or potential manipulation with possible litigation.

Adjustments may be made once a year or less often. The period between adjustments should be short for a gross lease but may be extended when the tenant pays most of the operating expenses. The degree of adjustment need not be the full change in the index selected; instead it may be a percentage of the change. For example, if 50% of the index were selected as the multiplier and the index rose by 20%, the rent would increase by 10%. This provides some protection to the landlord (who bought the property with pre-inflation dollars) but does not inflict the full brunt of inflation on the tenant.

Although a lease can require either the landlord or the tenant to pay property taxes, it is frequently appropriate for the tenant to pay such expenses for a single-tenant building. A compromise would use a *stop* (or *escalation*) *clause* whereby the tenant pays the increase in taxes over a base year amount, and the landlord pays the base year amount annually. When a net lease or a tax stop clause is used, there is less need for frequent rent adjustments.

There should be some penalty for a late rental payment, charge for attorneys' fees to cure delinquencies, and a landlord's lien on the property of a tenant who is delinquent in rent.

Tenants under a net lease may be expected to pay taxes, special assessments, and the like. No tenant should pay obligations of the landlord—such as income tax, gift, inheritance, franchise, or corporate tax, or a tax on the rental receipts of the landlord.

In an absolute net lease the tenant is responsible for maintenance, repairs, alterations, replacements, and

36

ERATING EXPENSES

ing expenses are those necessary to run invest-
erty even if it were bought without debt. The
uccessful investment is often spending money
operations. Being careful, but not skimping, is
r.

ng expenses may be divided into two cate-
ed expenses which do not change as the rate of
changes, and *variable expenses* which are
lated to the occupancy rate; as more people
d use a building, variable expenses increase.
xpenses include property taxes, license and
s, and property insurance. Variable expenses
nclude utilities (such as heat, water, sewer),
nt fees, payroll and payroll taxes, security,
g, advertising, and supplies and fees for varies provided by local government or private
. There may be a fixed component in
ormally classified as variable—for example,
d management cost regardless of the occu-

compare expenses reported for the subject
the experience of comparable properties.
nation may be obtained from published
rade organizations and also from property
ssessors, appraisers, and other professionals.
such as property taxes and energy costs, can
antially in a short time. You should consider
uation and underlying economic conditions
ng possible trends affecting expenditures.
ical costs of operation are examined, care
ken to assure that reporting practices have

improvements. This includes ordinary or extraordinary repairs, whether structural or nonstructural, interior or exterior.

However, even net leases of buildings require the landlord to be responsible for matters of structural integrity, such as the roof, exterior, and supporting walls, although nonstructural repairs and problems caused by a tenant's negligence are the tenant's responsibility.

The landlord should be required to remedy any malfunctions in the original building, including the heating, ventilation, and air conditioning system (HVAC), plumbing, and parking area. Curing any defects in the original construction should be an expense of the landlord. Manufacturers' warranties for appliances, especially the air conditioner compressor warranty length, should be specified in the lease as agreed by landlord and tenant. If the tenant does work on the building because of a defect that the landlord did not cure within a reasonable time, the tenant should be allowed to deduct the costs, plus interest, from future rent requirements.

Of utmost importance is the need to specify the obligations of each party; litigation is the typical result of a failure to do so.

35

PERCENTAGE LEASES

Leases with retail tenants are frequently percentage leases. They require either a fixed minimum rental or a percentage rent based on gross sales, whichever is greater. For example, rent for a 10,000-square-foot building may be $100,000 per year, plus 5% of sales above $2 million. Therefore, percentage rents are imposed only when sales exceed $2 million, which is $200 per square foot of floor area. Guidelines of typical sales per square foot for that retail business are often used as the base rate in the formula.

The advantage of a percentage lease to the tenant is a fair base rent and additional rent is paid only if the business volume justifies it. For the landlord, the percentage lease provides a reward for additional business due to LOCATION. This gives a landlord incentive to maintain a superior facility.

Percentage leases are commonplace in shopping malls. Different types of businesses have different percentage rates, even within the same mall. A firm selling luxury items, such as jewelry, tends to have a high markup and low inventory turnover compared with a grocery or discount store, which has a small profit but a high volume of sales. Smaller stores tend to pay a higher percentage than large national department stores, which are needed as anchor tenants to enable the shopping center to be financed. The percentage is often based on how much the store benefits from being within the mall. It can draw customers without spending money to advertise. Publications from the International Council of Shopping Centers and the Urban Land Institute provide a wealth of information regarding leasing and operating costs.

With a *straight-percentag* centage of the gross income imum or guaranteed rent; th

In a *variable scale le* according to the volume of centage rate might be 6% o and 4% on all sales abov converse arrangement is a overage increases as sa because the tenant's cost the sales volume, so the l of higher gross sales due

Certain lease provisio ness to both parties in a Monthly and/or annual the landlord may have fee is paid by the tenan

Typical Percentage Lease Ra Centers For Vario

Firm Type
Automotive
Bakery
Cards and gift
Furniture
Hardware
Jewelry
Liquor and w
Menswear
Paint, wallpa
Restaurant
Shoes
Sporting goc
Supermarket
Variety store

*Adapted from *Dollars an*

OP

Opera ment pro key to a wisely fo the answe Operati gories: *fix* occupancy directly re occupy an Fixed e permit fee generally manageme landscapin ous servic contractor expenses n a basic fix pancy rate. You may property to This infor reports of managers, a Some items change subs the local sit in forecasti When histor should be ta

100

been consistent throughout the period. (For instance, in one year the owner might have paid all utilities; but in the next, a separate metering system was installed so that tenants began to pay some.)

Replacement Reserve. Provision must be made for the replacement of short-lived items (such as carpeting, appliances, and some mechanical equipment) that wear out. These expenditures usually occur in large lump sums; a portion of the expected cost can be set aside every year to stabilize the expenses. A replacement reserve is necessary because the wearing out of short-lived assets causes a hidden loss of income. If this economic fact is not included in financial statements, the net operating income will be overstated. You should provide for a replacement reserve even though most owners do not actually set aside money for this purpose. (Note that the replacement reserve is not deductible from taxable income. The tax deduction occurs after the asset is replaced and the replacement is depreciated.) For example, appliances in an apartment unit cost $1,000 and have a ten-year expected life. A $100-per-year replacement reserve would be appropriate to fund this item. Reserves for carpet replacement are also appropriate.

The potential list of operating expenses for gross leased real estate includes:

Property taxes
    City
    County
    School district
    Special assessments

Insurance
    Hazard
    Liability

Utilities
    Telephone/Internet service
    Water
    Sewer or sewage disposal

Electricity
Gas

Administrative
    Management fees
    Clerical staff
    Maintenance staff
    Payroll taxes
    Legal and accounting expenses

Repairs and Maintenance
    Paint
    Decoration
    Carpet replacement
    Appliance repairs and replacement
    Supplies
    Gardening/landscaping
    Paving
    Roofing

Advertising and Promotion
    Media
    Business organization

Real estate investors may become successful by seeking ways to reduce expenses. Donald Trump's father was a legendary penny-pinching apartment owner in Queens, one of the five boroughs of New York City. Tired of buying a cleaning solvent used to mop hallway floors for a few dollars per gallon, he reportedly hired a chemist to analyze its composition. Then the senior Trump bought the raw ingredients at a substantial savings and mixed the products himself.

A major area for savings that is often overlooked is to appeal property taxes. Get good data concerning income or comparable sales or assessments of other property and visit the tax assessor or collector. The results can be very worthwhile.

37

MANAGING THE INVESTMENT

Managing an investment is altogether different from managing property, just as investing in securities differs from running the business that the securities represent.

Major functions of sound investment management are to:

- assure competent property management,
- determine the adequacy of the return and opportunities for improvement,
- review financial obligations,
- provide income tax planning, and
- develop an investment strategy.

Assuring Competent Property Management. You should select a local property manager to physically view the property, listen and act on tenant concerns, and assure compliance with the lease. The property manager is also responsible for arranging repairs; curing infractions of local government codes; and making sure that tax assessments are reasonable, insurance is adequate, and these functions are performed on time. He or she is the middleman, acting as a buffer between you and the property. Providing regular reports is one of the most important functions of a property manager. A good reporting form is comprehensive, yet simple and clear.

As an investor, you could manage the property yourself. But if you delegate that function, try to find a manager who is competent and who shares your values. For example, a certain property manager may seek to maintain high resale values for the property by redecorating frequently, whereas you may want to enhance current cash flow and would defer some maintenance to achieve that goal. Convey your desires to the manager and periodically check that they're being followed.

Property managers offer different levels of technical and personal skills, and different levels of experience. Experience as an apartment manager does not necessarily guarantee expertise in managing a freestanding store. When hiring a property manager, you should check for the adequacy and consistency of education and experience. The Certified Property Manager (CPM) designation is offered by the Institute of Real Estate Management (IREM), an affiliate of the National Association of Realtors. The Certified Shopping Center Manager (CSCM) designation is offered by the International Council of Shopping Centers. Professional designations from recognized organizations indicate a relatively high level of expertise and professionalism in a property manager.

Determining the Adequacy of Return and Opportunities for Improvement. At least once a year (a good time is after completing income tax return information), the investor should determine the rate of cash flow from the property. This may be defined in any or all of at least three ways: (1) cash flow before subtracting debt service, divided by the estimated property value, (2) cash flow after debt service, divided by the value of equity, and/or (3) cash flow after both debt service and income taxes, divided by equity value.

These should provide positive rates of return that exceed bank CDs or dividends on common stock. Compared to bank CDs, the real estate should provide added returns for risk and illiquidity. Real estate investors often accept a reduced current return when appreciation in value is expected to be received in the future. Appreciation may be very important, although the investor must understand that the increase in value is less valuable than the same amount of current cash flow because of the time value of money.

Reviewing Financial Obligations. Investors need to be mindful that short-term loans on the property and large expenses, such as real estate taxes and insurance, must be met or the property may be lost. Just when things seem to be going well, a tenant may unexpectedly vacate, or an unexpected large expense can materialize. A prudent investor should keep some reserves because such surprises are rarely positive.

Providing Income Tax Planning. As a real estate portfolio may grow with appreciation and new acquisitions, an investor needs to plan for the effect on income taxes. Perhaps dwindling depreciation tax deductions will cause rising income taxes, or increasing acquisitions will result in opportunities to gain from tax shelter. Although death may not be on an investor's mind, a family succession plan or adequate cash to pay estate taxes may be required to keep a portfolio intact.

Developing an Investment Strategy. It is always useful to develop an investment strategy to help provide guidance when opportunities appear. A plan can be useful when there is an opportunity to purchase another property; you must understand how it fits into your overall investment strategy. The same is true when an offer is made that allows an investor to sell a property. Such a plan, or at least a thought process, can be modified as one ages and market conditions change.

38

INSURANCE

Insurance is a way to spread the RISK of a potential hazard among those who might experience the unwanted event. It is a way to transfer risk from each individual to a large group that is better able to absorb a loss. Real estate owners face many hazards, some of which are insurable. Fire is a common hazard, and extended coverage may also include: losses due to lightning, hail, explosion, windstorm, tornado, cyclone, riot, disorder or civil commotion, aircraft damage, vehicle damage, smoke damage, vandalism, and malicious mischief; also war if the United States is engaged in hostilities; and boiler explosion insurance (if a steam boiler is used), plate glass insurance, and sprinkler leakage insurance.

To guard against likely losses, you should carry ample insurance but not excessive amounts that involve additional costs and reimbursement limits. *Title insurance* requires a one-time fee to protect against title defects. A lender will require it to the extent of the loan; additional amounts are optional. *Hazard insurance* is required to the extent of the loan amount, and more is highly desirable when the equity is substantial, as described below. *Rent interruption insurance* is often desirable. In the event of a fire, the mortgage payment must be met while the property is being rebuilt, even though you have no rental income.

When arranging insurance, the owner often recognizes that a complete loss is unlikely because something of value will remain in all but the worst disasters. Therefore good business judgment is to insure only a fraction—say 50% of the property value. However, hazard insurance policies have a *coinsurance requirement* level, usually 80%, whereby the insurance company reimburses only part of any loss if the insurance was not 80% of the property's replacement cost. For example, suppose a special use building is worth $900,000, excluding land, but it will take $1 million to replace it. If insurance carried is under $800,000 (80% of $1 million), the insurer will reimburse only a fraction of any loss. If $500,000 is carried, the reimbursement is 50%/80% of a loss, up to a maximum of $500,000. Consequently, you must be conscious of the adequacy of insurance in relation to the coinsurance requirement. In addition, the amount of insurance should be based on *replacement cost* rather than MARKET VALUE.

Liability insurance is a crucial concern. You are liable for a hazardous condition even though you didn't cause it or know of it. A broken step, patch of ice, or wet hallway can cause serious injury and expensive litigation for which you may be liable. Today, $300,000 or more of liability coverage may be considered barely adequate for some properties, especially where there is mechanical equipment such as an escalator or automatic door opener.

Apartment complexes or motels with swimming pools may have special insurance needs to be covered. A diving board may add thousands to a liability insurance policy, but the owner who fails to insure it is assuming great risk.

Larger property owners may carry insurance to protect against failure of mechanical equipment, such as refrigeration units in restaurants, air-conditioning compressors, boilers, escalators, and elevators. Service contracts may be used in conjunction with or in lieu of this kind of insurance.

Deductible amounts are important in reducing premiums. The deductible is the amount you must pay for each loss; the higher the deductible, the lower the premium. Ask an insurance agent for rates based on different levels of deductibles, and select the one that offers the best compromise between cost and protection.

For property owned in a PARTNERSHIP or other co-ownership arrangement, each partner may have *life insurance* on the other. If one dies, the survivor receives enough to buy out the interest of the heirs so the business may continue. Otherwise the result may be a forced sale of the entire property.

Insurance is generally not available for poor business conditions, increased competition, or the failure of a tenant. But a prudent owner will protect against risks that are insurable at a reasonable cost.

39

REDUCED PARTICIPATION AND REDUCED RISK

There are many decisions that must be made in the course of building and maintaining a portfolio of real estate investments. Having a central strategy that fits your goals and taste for risk will be a big help in making these decisions in a consistent manner. Your strategy will help you determine what types of assets to acquire and when to acquire and dispose of assets.

While there are many different ways to devise a strategy, most will fall somewhere along two fundamental scales: level of risk exposure and level of participation.

Although all investment involves some risk, some investors wish to minimize those risks while others are willing to take much higher risks in pursuit of their goals. It is possible, even within a real estate portfolio, to vary the level of risk to a great degree. Much depends on the type of property acquired. Undeveloped land is inherently more risky than a fully leased-up building with high-quality tenants. Risk can also be altered by the time horizon adopted for holding a property. Conservative investors generally look to hold a property for a long time—ten or more years—whereas a high-risk investor will want to turn over properties much more rapidly. A conservative investor will look for properties that will hold their value and produce a good cash flow stream over the long term. An aggressive investor looks for properties with relatively short-term potential—those that can be turned over for a profit.

The other dimension to consider is the level of participation. Real estate is usually thought of as an investment that takes a lot of hands-on involvement. But you can own properties and hire out the management duties. You can own property indirectly through a partnership or REIT and have no management responsibilities whatsoever.

Your strategy needs to fit you. Conservative investors often start out with a stock, bond, or CD portfolio that they want to diversify, enhance, or expand by adding real estate to the mix. They choose properties according to a "buy and hold" approach based on acquiring quality properties at relatively good prices and holding them for the long term. One goal of such investors may be to own a group of income-producing properties debt-free by the time they retire. They might favor a portfolio that performs like an annuity, throwing off cash at a consistent and uniform rate. At the same time, they appreciate the inflation-hedging abilities of such a portfolio.

Aggressive investors see real estate as an opportunity to build wealth quickly by exploiting inefficiencies in the market. They look for properties that are heavily discounted in the market and try to overcome whatever it is that buyers do not like about the property. Maybe it needs some renovation, attractive financing, or some marketing skill. Some investors buy up land in the path of growth and hold it until development is imminent. Others might take a chance on older areas turning around. To this type of investor, the possibility of quick profits offsets the risk of failure. Hotels and office buildings tend to be more affected by national economic conditions than are apartments and industrial properties.

The participation choice may be based on the amount of time an investor has to give. Some investors are full time and can afford to spend their days managing property. Others have a day job and are limited in how much time they can devote. There are other considerations as well. An investor may not want to share decision making with a partner or manager. She may have expertise in operating certain kinds of property. In these instances, she may want to take an active role.

On the other hand, passive investments tend to be more liquid. Shares of an actively traded REIT or an ETF can be sold quickly in the stock market, whereas a building may take months to sell. A passive investor can own shares in several different assets, thereby diversifying among property types and locations. An active investor may have all his money in one property. Active investment is most appropriate for those who wish to invest in the local area and know the territory. It may be difficult to find passive investments that specialize in the locality.

Although your level of risk tolerance and participation are separate issues, they combine to determine the types of assets appropriate for your portfolio. A conservative active investor will look for properties with proven income production and good prospects for retaining their value. Likewise, a conservative passive investor might buy a REIT with a competitive dividend yield but little or no leverage. An aggressive active investor, on the other hand, might seek out undeveloped land in the path of a city's growth or a distressed property with turnaround potential. An aggressive passive investor might speculate in mortgage derivatives or short-sell stocks of homebuilders or brokerage firms when it appears that a turn in the market is imminent.

	ACTIVE (HANDS-ON PROPERTY)	PASSIVE (NO PROPERTY MANAGEMENT)
HIGH RISK	Buy undeveloped land Buy hotels Buy before rezoning Buy environmentally impaired Buy for immediate resale (flip)	Sell short: stocks, REITs Buy syndication Buy/sell options Buy on margin
LOW RISK	Buy fully occupied: • Apartments • Industrial buildings	Buy conservative dividend-paying stocks, REITS Buy real estate mutual funds

40

LIMITED LIABILITY COMPANIES (LLCs) AND PARTNERSHIPS

A group of investors may band together to purchase a property that is too large or expensive for a single one to afford. There are various forms of business organization that may accommodate ownership.

Although limited liability companies (LLCs) were developed relatively recently (since about 1990 in most states), they have quickly become the dominant, preferred form for individuals. An LLC is a distinct type of business that offers an alternative to partnerships and corporations by combining the corporate advantages of limited liability with the advantage of pass-through taxation offered by a sole proprietorship or partnership.

LLCs offer numerous advantages over other forms of ownership. These include:

• **Pass-through taxation.** The earnings of an LLC are taxed only once. They are treated like the earnings of partnerships, sole proprietorships, and most S Corporations.

• **Limited liability.** The LLC owner's liability is generally limited to the amount of money the person has invested in the LLC. Thus, LLC members are offered the same limited-liability protection as a corporation's shareholders.

• **Flexible management structure and ownership.** Like general partnerships, LLCs are generally free to establish any organization structure agreed on by the members. Thus, profit interests may be separated from voting interests.

To form an LLC, articles of organization must be prepared and filed with the state, and filing fees, initial franchise taxes, and other initial fees must be paid. An attorney should be employed for assurance, though there is not a legal requirement to do so.

Partnerships are a popular way to invest in real estate. A *partnership* is formed when two or more investors agree to purchase and operate property. All expenses, income, tax deductions, and liability are shared among the partners, generally in accordance with the percentage each owns. However, income and management responsibilities may be allocated among partners in a variety of ways. The partnership is normally not a tax-paying unit. Instead, it serves as a conduit—all of the income or loss is typically passed through to the partners. This overcomes the problem of double taxation on income such as that faced by a corporation (the firm pays tax on earnings, then shareholders pay tax on dividends). A *joint venture* is like a partnership, but is formed for just one business transaction. A *tenancy in common* is when multiple owners each own a share of the property, as distinguished from owning a partnership interest. (Lawyers will explain that the difference can be crucial.)

Partnerships may be structured to provide limited liability to some of its partners. A *limited partnership* designates one or more partners as *general partners* who accept all liability and make most of the decisions on managing the investment. Limited partners are liable only to the extent of their actual investment. However, the general partner may request additional investment contributions if the venture runs into trouble. Limited partnerships that have too many characteristics of a corporation will be taxed as a corporation. In addition, investors in limited partnerships that own real estate may not offset partnership losses against other income.

In most cases, the general partner is a *syndicator* who organizes the partnership and accepts fees for his or her services. The limited partners are passive investors. Limited partnerships may be small or large. Each partner is required to put in a certain amount of cash that is used to purchase property. The partnership may take out mortgage loans or buy with cash. It may buy only one property or have extensive holdings. Some partnerships identify properties only after they have raised cash. These are called *blind pools*. In most cases, a partnership will specialize in one type of investment situation, such as subsidized housing, undeveloped land, or motel franchises.

Interests in a partnership are often hard to sell. In some cases, a change in partners will dissolve a partnership. Transfers of ownership often must have the approval of all other partners. This problem may be resolved with a *master limited partnership*. These ventures are more like large, closed-end funds. Shares may be traded readily through securities brokers.

The basic problems with partnerships are the lack of control exercised by the investor and the high fees charged by many syndicators. Also, because most syndicated partnerships are based on a specialized investment strategy, their performance is based on the success of that approach. Many older limited partnerships were based on tax shelter and are not structured in a currently viable form. Indeed, many of these older partnerships have been acquired, at deeply discounted prices, by real estate investment trusts (see CORPORATIONS AND REAL ESTATE INVESTMENT TRUSTS/41). Nevertheless, partnerships can be a good way for a passive investor to get involved in real estate. Despite high fees, many partnerships provide attractive returns.

41

CORPORATIONS AND REAL ESTATE INVESTMENT TRUSTS

The corporate form of ownership allows you to get income from business activity without exposing yourself to personal liability. In other words, as a stockholder, you can only lose what you invest in the stock. Unlike PARTNERSHIPS, corporations may buy and sell properties and change stockholders without dissolving and reforming. Therefore, stockholders can sell their shares readily. The corporation also enjoys a perpetual life, whereas partnerships must have a finite life.

The major problem with corporations is that they are taxed twice: first on income they produce and second, shareholders must pay tax on any dividends. In addition, corporate losses cannot be passed through to the shareholders. This makes the corporate form inappropriate for most real estate investment situations.

An **S Corporation** enjoys some of the benefits of both the corporation and partnership forms. Shareholder liability is limited to what they have invested, similar to the corporate form. However, income of the corporation is taxed only once, as personal income to the shareholders. To qualify under Subchapter S, the corporation must limit the maximum number of shareholders to 75 and follow other rules specified by the tax code. An S Corporation may be appropriate for some types of investment such as speculation in undeveloped land, land development, or mineral exploration.

Real estate investment trusts were allowed by tax law to encourage real estate investment without the negative tax provisions of corporation.

Buying a share in a real estate investment trust, or REIT (pronounced "reet"), is like buying a share of stock in a company that owns real estate. The share can be bought and sold on the stock exchange or over the counter. This provides liquidity to the real estate investment. Your risk is limited to the price of the shares you buy. If the REIT gets into trouble, no one can make claims on other property you may own. You can get the advantages of professional management of the portfolio of properties and diversification among many properties.

Among the disadvantages is the fact that you don't have any input to the buying and selling of the properties owned by the REIT. Also, you can't use losses from DEPRECIATION — TAX to offset other income. However, such losses have been greatly reduced by tax reform, so this is not much of a disadvantage.

Unlike corporations that own some real property, REITs are required to invest at least 75% of their funds in real estate. So owning shares of a REIT is a good substitute for investing directly in real estate. Most REITs distribute virtually all of their earnings to shareholders. They are required to distribute at least 95% to avoid taxation at the REIT level. (This restriction limits REITs' growth potential and sometimes forces them to use debt financing for acquisitions.) Therefore, they pay a relatively high dividend compared to price and can be a good choice for investors who need current income. Of course, shareholders must pay tax on these earnings.

REITs tend to specialize. Some purchase properties and are called *equity REITs*. Others buy or make permanent loans and construction loans on real estate. These are called *mortgage REITs*. Still others have both types of assets and are called *hybrid REITs*.

REITs were formed to allow small investors to get involved with real estate. Shares often sell for a few dollars and commission rates are the same as for stocks. Since they sell on major stock exchanges, they can be purchased through discount and on-line brokers.

They were a very popular investment in the early 1970s. Many mistakes were made by REIT managers during that era as they attempted to find a place for so much money. The recession of the mid-1970s brought an end to the REIT craze and share prices plunged. They enjoyed renewed popularity in the late 1980s as tax reform destroyed tax shelter opportunities for passive investors. Their high yields made REITs a hot investment in the mid-1990s and they assumed their place in well-diversified portfolios.

Many of the larger mutual fund groups—Vanguard, Fidelity, and others—offer funds devoted to real estate. These funds invest in REITs and real estate-related stocks, such as major real estate developers. These funds can be good choices for investors who want to put money into real estate but do not want to research individual REITs or companies.

While a mutual fund allows you to spread your investment among several firms and not be dependent on a single manager, it reduces your ability to manage your tax liability. If a mutual fund has capital gains from trading securities, it must distribute them to shareholders, who, in turn, must pay taxes on that income. You can get the diversification advantages of a mutual fund without this problem by buying exchange-traded funds (ETFs). These closed-end funds trade just like individual stocks. You don't realize capital gains until you sell the shares. For investors in higher tax brackets, this feature can be very attractive.

42

ANALYZING, BUYING, AND MONITORING REITs

Public REITs are sold over the major stock exchanges just like common stocks (private REITs of limited size and liquidity are also available). That means an investor can acquire these assets as easily as buying shares of General Electric. In addition, REITs are easy to monitor since their market price is reported every time there is a trade. These characteristics make REITs an ideal way to invest in real estate for those who do not have the time or inclination to own real property directly. There are some things an investor should know about REITs to better understand which ones to acquire and when to sell.

Not all REITs are the same. Rather, they tend to specialize in certain types of property (apartments, office buildings), regions (southeastern United States, California), or market segments (starter homes, retirement communities). An excellent resource for information about REITs is the web site maintained by the National Association of Real Estate Investment Trusts (*www.nareit.com*). At this site you can search a list of REITs for the types of property they own and for the states in which the properties are located. For example, if you want to invest in apartments or properties located in Arizona, you can use the site to search for specific REITs that match your profile. Also, through the Yahoo search engine you can find the stock market ticker symbol for each REIT and order annual reports.

Like stocks, REITs can be used to implement your basic investment strategy. You may acquire individual REITs when you think they are underpriced using a value investment approach. Or you may employ a quality strategy to pick highly rated REITs with a long track record of dividends and earnings growth. You may buy REITs to diversify a portfolio by allocating a certain percentage of your holdings to real estate. Or you may want to shift into and out of REITs as the real estate market rises and falls (or at least as you perceive and expect that it will). Keep in mind that academic studies question whether real estate stocks follow real estate markets very well. Some have found that REITs perform just like any other small cap stock. Lately, REITs have enjoyed favor among investors at times when commercial real estate was underperforming. This was due largely to the fact that REITs offered high dividend yields compared with alternative investments. In this regard, some REITs performed like utility stocks.

How you buy stocks may also depend on your investment strategy. A contrarian value investor may want to use a discount stockbroker, doing the research and picking stocks on her own. A growth-oriented investor may want to rely on a full-service broker to provide reports and suggest individual stocks. A much more passive approach is available in the form of real estate mutual funds, which hold diversified portfolios of REITs and other real estate–related stocks. Look for analysis and evaluation of these mutual funds in the publications offered by Morningstar.

Here are some things to consider in evaluating individual REIT issues:

• **Dividends.** REITs are required to pay out almost all of their income in the form of dividends to shareholders. Therefore, all REITs pay dividends. The dividend yield rate is the ratio of annual dividend income to the current value of the REIT and is comparable to the dividend yield of other stocks or the current yield of a bond—giving you a ready indicator to compare individual REITs as well as other asset types. Because REITs must pay out most of their earnings, their potential to grow in value is largely limited to increases in the value of their holdings or changes in their popularity in the stock market. Some may generate more funds from operations (FFO) than they must pay in dividends, so that may provide a source of growth. Dividends, however, may increase or decrease as income from the portfolio changes. Keep in mind that REIT dividends are taxable in the year in which they are distributed, and, unlike other stocks, REITs are not subject to the reduced rates intended to offset some of the double taxation of stock dividends.[1] A good risk indicator is the track record of a REIT's past payout of dividends.

• **Earnings per Share.** Check the last several years of earnings per share to see how a REIT is faring. There may be seasonal variation in earnings, so compare like quarters (first quarter 2010 to first quarter 2011) to get a proper trendline. Compare these patterns to other REITs or to an index of REITs (reported by *nareit.com*) to see if any problems are specific to the REIT or are going through the whole market.

• **P/E Ratio.** The price-to-earnings ratio tells you what the market is willing to pay for the earnings produced by the REIT. You can compare an individual REIT to the whole market using the P/E. Interpreting this indicator depends on your philosophy of the market and outlook for the real estate market. A high P/E may indicate that investors think the company has a great future of growing income production, or it may just be overpriced if you feel that optimism is misplaced. A low P/E may indicate an overlooked value or a company that is milking a portfolio of deteriorating properties. Either

---

[1]REIT distributions may include some capital gains and return of capital which receive preferential tax treatment.

way, you can use P/E ratios to screen REITs for further investigation. Growth investors might look for high P/Es whereas value investors seek out low P/Es.

• **Net Asset Value.** The current market value of the properties held by a REIT offers a fundamental value indicator. If an estimate is made of what the portfolio of properties is worth, the total is netted out against any debt owed by the REIT. This, in essence, indicates what the REIT would be worth if it were liquidated. By comparing the share price to the net asset value per share, you can calculate a premium (or discount if it is negative) placed on the firm's management. Depending on your investment outlook and style, you may want to maximize or minimize this premium.

43

BECOMING A REAL ESTATE LENDER

You can be a real estate investor without actually owning real property. Instead of taking an ownership position, you may want to bankroll someone else willing to take on those responsibilities. You will be freed from the tasks of finding and acquiring properties, as well as operating or developing the properties. However, you still will need to understand what makes a good real estate investment, since you will be supplying most of the money for such investments. If the investment is a success, you will have the advantage of getting paid first. However, the amount you are paid does not depend on how successful the investment turns out to be. If the investment is not successful, you may not get paid at all, but you will have access to the property through fore-closure.

There are several ways the small, active investor can get involved in real estate lending. You might make first, junior, or interim loans for commercial properties that are of a lower quality level than is acceptable to estab-lished institutional lenders. You might buy mortgages that home sellers took as part of the sales price. These often are second mortgages used to reduce the down payment required to assume an existing mortgage loan. You may decide to offer sub-prime lending to those with poor or unestablished credit ratings who want to buy a home. You can also lend to developers, builders, and remodelers.

You may even decide to become a mortgage banker or broker. This option is especially appropriate for investors who are active but do not have a great deal of capital. A mortgage banker uses her capital to make loans that can be sold in the secondary market. By doing so, she recoups her funds to make more loans, hopefully deriving profits in the process as well as fees for servicing the loans. A mortgage broker connects borrowers with lenders, earning a fee when such a connection takes place. Mortgage brokers help borrowers find loans appropriate for their situation but do not service loans.

Here are some things to consider prior to taking on the role of lender:

• **What will be the source of your capital?** Buying whole loans ties up a lot of cash and makes it difficult to diversify. Mortgage banking allows you to replenish your capital when the loans are sold. Mortgage brokerage requires relatively little cash. You may be able to raise capital through borrowing, hoping to earn a higher yield on your portfolio than your cost of funds. Keep in mind that any mismatch in the maturity of your assets and liabilities exposes you to risk.

• **What types of properties will you finance?** Commercial properties are considered more risky than owner-occupied homes. Development lending is riskier than lending on improved properties already producing cash flow. You may want to lend only for types of properties you understand or in which you have adequate business experience.

• **What will you require to approve a loan?** If you are selling the loans in the secondary market, you will need to find out and satisfy the demands of the eventual buyer of the loans. Otherwise, you will need to develop criteria corresponding to the level of quality you desire. Keep in mind that the higher the security required, the lower the yield you will be able to demand.

• **What are the laws governing mortgage loans and loan origination?** A substantial amount of federal and state law has developed pertaining to the home mortgage business. Truth in Lending and the Real Estate

Settlement Procedures Act are the most invasive, but there are a lot of new laws concerning lending practices. Commercial lending is less restrictive, but you need to become familiar with basic laws governing the conduct of business in your state.

• **What is your recourse if the borrower defaults?** The common satisfaction for a default is foreclosure of the borrower's rights under the mortgage. You may acquire the property or allow it to be sold and attach the proceeds. Mortgage documents must be clear, as well as consistent with state law, on how you may respond to a default.

• **What will you need to do to enter this business?** You will need some type of office arrangement. If you originate loans, you will need a way to attract and accommodate borrowers. You may need to advertise in some way. You may want to incorporate to avoid personal liability in case the business is unsuccessful. To enter the mortgage banking or brokerage business you will need to establish relationships with real estate brokers, lenders, or mortgage investors. In some cases, you may need to be licensed.

44

CALCULATING THE VALUE OF A LOAN

When buying loans, you will need to discount the loan in order to achieve the yield you require. To do this, you need to know how the interest rate charged on the loan affects its discounted value. Once you calculate the value of the loan discounted at your required yield, you know how much to offer for the loan or how many discount points to charge for making the loan.

As a first example, suppose you make a $100,000 loan at a 7% face interest per year. How many discount points would you have to charge if you require the loan to yield 8%? You will need to make an assumption about how long the loan will survive before it is repaid. If the loan goes to maturity (for example, 30 years), you can calculate its value on a financial calculator:

1. Enter the maturity [360 months] in the "N" button.
2. Enter the face interest rate [7%] in the "I" button. You may need to divide by 12 months.
3. Enter the principal [$100,000] in the "PV" button.
4. Press the "PMT" button to get the monthly payment [$665.30 of principal and interest]. Save this number in memory.
5. Again, enter the maturity in the "N" button.
6. Enter your required yield [8%] in the "I" button (divide by 12 to convert to a monthly rate).
7. Recall the monthly payment from memory [665.30] and enter it in the "PMT" button.
8. Press the "PV" button to get the present value of the loan payments [$90,670]. You can pay $90,670 to get an 8% yield rate for a loan with a $100,000 principal at a 7% face rate.

9. Divide the present value by the amount of the loan [90,670 ÷ 100,000 = .9067].
10. Subtract this ratio from 1 [1 − .9067 = .0933] and multiply by 100 to get the number of discount points needed to raise the yield to your requirement [100 × .0933 = 9.33 points].

So you will need to charge 9.33 discount points to get the yield to 8%. Most loans do not go to maturity because they are refinanced or paid off when the home changes hands or defaults. Suppose you expect the loan to be paid off in 10 years. The monthly payments of principal and interest will be the same as calculated above. However, you need to calculate the outstanding loan balance after 10 years:

1. Enter the remaining term after the 10 years has elapsed [360 months − 120 months = 240 months] in the "N" button.
2. Enter the face interest rate [7% divided by 12] in the "I" button.
3. Enter the monthly payment [665.30] in the "PMT" button.
4. Press the "PV" button to get the balance after 10 years [$85,812].

The present value of the loan is the sum of the discounted value of ten years of payments plus the present value of the repaid loan balance:

1. Enter the term [120] in the "N" button.
2. Enter the required yield [8% divided by 12] in the "I" button.
3. Enter the monthly payment [665.30] in the "PMT" button.
4. Press the "PV" button and save the results in memory [$54,832].
5. Clear the financial registers.
6. Enter the expected term [120] again in the "N" button.

7. Enter the required yield [8% divided by 12] in the "I" button.
8. Enter the balance [85,812] in the "FV" button.
9. Press the "PV" button to get the present value of the balance after 10 years [$38,660].
10. Add this amount to the present value of the 10 years of payments you stored in memory to get the value of the loan [$38,660 + $54,832 = $93,492].
11. You will need to charge 6.5 points to get your yield of 8% if you project the loan to be paid back in 10 years. Because you bought at a discount from face value, any repayment before that time increases your expected yield.

For a second example, suppose you can buy a second mortgage from someone who just sold a home with seller financing. The loan amount is $20,000 and calls for 10 years of monthly payments at a 6% face interest rate. The loan is self-amortizing. How much can you offer for the loan if your required yield is 8%?

First calculate the monthly payment:

1. Enter the term [120] in the "N" button.
2. Enter the face interest rate [6% divided by 12] in the "I" button.
3. Enter the loan amount [20,000] in the "PV" button.
4. Press the "PMT" button to get the monthly payment [$222].

Now calculate the value of the payments discounted at your required yield rate:

1. Clear financial registers.
2. Enter the term [120] in the "N" button.
3. Enter the yield [8% divided by 12] in the "I" button.
4. Enter the monthly payment [$222] in the "PMT" button.

5. Press the "PV" button to get the present value of the loan [$18,298].

The present value at your required yield is the most you can pay for the loan and still achieve this yield. Anytime you pay less than face value, your yield will be higher than the face interest rate.

45

INVESTING IN REAL ESTATE DEBT SECURITIES

Most people do not think of bonds as real estate assets. However, there are several types of bonds that provide financing for people to buy homes and rental properties, as well as other real estate activities. Adding these assets to your portfolio is considered a type of real estate investment.

Here is a brief description of the major types of real estate debt securities:

• **GNMA (Ginnie Mae) Pass-throughs.** The Government National Mortgage Association, called Ginnie Mae in mortgage lingo, is an agency of the federal government that guarantees pools of mortgage loans. These "pools" are loans on houses that are grouped together and owned by private companies. Debt securities are sold to investors who gain the right to all interest and principal payments received from the loans in the pool. Ginnie Mae's guarantee makes these securities more marketable and minimizes the risk that investors will lose their principal should the mortgages go into default. However, the maturity of the pass-through is uncertain, as all principal repayments are passed on to investors. This feature limits the upside potential of the investment, since homeowners will tend to refinance the loans when interest rates go down. Unfortunately, the value of the security falls when interest rates go up, just like that of any other fixed-rate bond.

- **Freddie Mac PCs.** The Federal Home Loan Mortgage Corporation, or Freddie Mac, is a shareholder-owned company created by the federal government to organize a secondary market for conventional mortgage loans. One of the ways that Freddie Mac does this is to buy loans from mortgage bankers and lending institutions and form pools of like-kind loans (for example, a pool of fixed-rate home loans). Investors in these pools receive "participation certificates" (PCs) entitling them to share in the cash flow generated by the pool. Cash flow consists of both interest and principal, so that the pool dissipates as loans are repaid and refinanced. Many of the mortgages in the pools are insured against loss to some extent.

- **Fannie Mae Mortgage-Backed Securities.** The Federal National Mortgage Association is yet another entity created by the federal government to help foster a secondary market in home loans. Like Freddie Mac, Fannie Mae is shareholder owned.[1] However, Fannie Mae was at one time an agency of the federal government. When Fannie Mae went private, Ginnie Mae was formed to assume the duties of Fannie Mae that could not be expected to earn profits. Today, both Freddie Mac and Fannie Mae are highly profitable companies and buy more than three-fourths of all the home loans originated in the country. Like the other securities described above, the Fannie Mae mortgage-backed securities (MBSs) are backed by a pool of home loans, many of which contain VA or FHA guarantees, and pay regular distributions based on the cash flow generated by the pool.

- **Collateralized Mortgage Obligations (CMOs).** These are securities backed by pools of mortgage loans owned by lending institutions or private secondary market investors. CMOs offer a series of investor classes—called "tranches"—of varying maturities. Essentially,

---

[1] Both these entities are currently under conservatorship of the federal government but continue to operate much as they have previously.

133

the tranches are organized in a hierarchy based on priority of payments made on the loans in the pool. Therefore, the tranch that has first priority will mature first. This feature allows investors to select the maturity they prefer. Longer-term tranches usually command higher yields because of their deferred payout periods.

• **Mortgage REITs.** These securities are structured just like the equity REITs described in Key 41. Instead of buying real properties, however, these REITs make mortgage and construction loans backed by real properties. Mortgage REITs tend to be regarded as riskier than their equity counterparts, especially when they are supported by construction loans. More than likely, that perception is a holdover from the 1970s, when mortgage REITs made a lot of high-risk development loans that never repaid.

It may be impractical for most investors to buy these securities directly, since they often require a large minimum investment ($25,000 or more). However, many of them may be purchased through mutual funds organized by major fund families.

Bonds are issued with a stated, fixed coupon rate of interest. This rate is based on the amount of principal (the par or "face value") raised by the bond. For example, a bond with a face value of $1,000 and coupon interest rate of 5% pays $50 in interest each year, typically half of that every six months. A mortgage bond may, in addition, also pay back principal as the loans in the pool are repaid. However, principal payments are return *of* investment rather than return *on* investment. You are simply getting your money back early. When a bond is sold in the market, it is priced either at par or above (a premium) or below (a discount) the par value, based on how the coupon rate compares to the rate currently available on other assets of comparable risk. The premium or discount adjusts the yield on the bond to the market rate. Market value can change over time, as interest rates fluctuate, as the outlook for repayment of the loans changes, and as the bond approaches maturity (at which time investors will receive the par value less any principal already received).

Thus, there are several types of risk associated with debt securities. One is the risk that many of the loans will go into *default* and principal will be lost. This is not a serious risk with most mortgage-backed securities, since each loan is backed by a mortgage on a real property, many also carry mortgage insurance against default, and some of the debt issues are guaranteed by their sponsor. A second type of risk is *interest rate risk* associated with changes in market interest rates. Since most securities pay out at a fixed rate of interest, their market value depends on that rate being competitive with current rates. When market rates rise, security value falls; when rates fall, value goes up. This may mean that a premium paid for an issue can evaporate when interest rates rise. A third type of risk is *maturity risk*—getting your money back too quickly. This is a problem when market yields are falling because all principal returned must be reinvested at a lower yield. Unfortunately for investors, most mortgages allow borrowers to repay the loan at any time without penalty. When rates are falling and reinvestment opportunities are less lucrative, the probability of loan repayment is highest because borrowers will seek to lower their debt service by refinancing at the lower rates.

Fortunately, most mortgage-backed investments offer very competitive yields and are attractive to investors who want income and relative security (in the sense of low principal risk). They can be a good alternative to other, lower-yielding fixed-income investments and may provide a way for investors to hedge against other investments sensitive to interest rate change.

46

CONDOS, CO-OPS, AND TIME-SHARES

There are various ways of cutting up the ownership of real estate. This is often necessary to allow buyers with limited funds to enjoy the benefits of owning property to serve their needs. Some type of shared ownership is involved in these arrangements.

Condominium, or "condo," combines individual and collective ownership. The owner has title to a unit within a building or complex and shared ownership of the rest of the property. For example, in a high-rise condo apartment building, each owner controls a dwelling unit in the building. The hallways, elevators, lobby, grounds, and recreation areas are shared and owned in common among all unit owners. Each owner may finance his or her purchase with a separate mortgage loan and take any tax deductions from the property. Units can be sold just as any other property. There is some type of owner's association that collects fees to pay for maintenance and other costs connected with the common property. Condo owners are subject to a set of bylaws covering how the property may be used. Some condos restrict the ability of owners to rent out their units. Check the bylaws before buying.

A **co-op** is similar to a condo but the legal setup is different. A co-op property is owned by a special purpose corporation. Purchase of shares in the corporation allows use of a unit in the building. The costs of running the building, including debt service on the mortgage loan used to buy the building, are shared among shareholders. Shares in a unit may be sold on the market, but the corporation, by vote of the shareholders, can decide on who may occupy the unit. Therefore, shares in a co-op are not as liquid as units in a condo. Co-ops are used primarily for high-rise residential buildings, particularly in New York City.

One of the keys for an investor to make money on a co-op or condo is to buy at the initial offering of a new building or a conversion from a rental. Usually existing tenants are offered an "insider's" price, typically 25% less than the price offered to the market. A well-connected investor might be able to buy at an attractive price even if it is more than the insider's price. Proposed condominium developments are frequently presold to investors who put up only a nominal amount for each unit, but they stand to multiply gains with successful developments. Much depends on timing and risk. See "bubble markets" in the Q & A section. Undertaking a co-op or condo conversion or large development is usually the domain of active developers.

A **time-share** property allows individuals to buy the right to use a property for a certain period of the year. For example, you may buy the right to use a specific property for the first two weeks in July each year. Time-shares are most often used with vacation property. Some time-shares actually provide owners with title to the property, whereas others only provide a right to use the property. If the project runs into financial difficulty, owning title provides you with a stronger position in any settlement. Some projects are sold before completion. You should beware of promised facilities that may never be completed. Promoters also may claim that you can trade with other time-shares in other areas. However, there is no guaranteed right to exchange for a more desirable period or place on an even basis. Resales of time-shares are not well organized and may be difficult or impossible to arrange. Many feel that time-shares may provide good vacation opportunities but are poor investments because the price is high. For example, a unit that might sell for $200,000 as a condo might be broken into 50 weeks for $10,000 each, which totals $500,000. Potential profit for the developer is great.

47

CONTRACT
TO PURCHASE

An offer to buy investment real estate is usually submitted by a proposed contract. Key clauses in such a contract are:

Purchase price. How much is offered for the property.

Earnest, escrow, hand, or good faith money. Shows seriousness on the buyer's part and will be forfeited if the contract is signed by both parties but the buyer cannot consummate the purchase. Most contracts specify that if the purchaser cannot arrange the financing specified in the contract, or the property does not pass requirements for its condition as stated in the contract, or the seller cannot deliver marketable title, the deal is off and all of the earnest money must be refunded.

Financing terms. How the buyer will pay for the property. This must describe any proposed loan from the seller and any required loans from third parties. Loans to be obtained from third parties should be described as to the expected source, maximum acceptable interest rate, minimum acceptable principal, and other characteristics. If the buyer cannot arrange the required loan(s), he or she is generally not required to forfeit the earnest money.

Deposit increase. Conditions under which the buyer must increase the earnest money to maintain the contract.

Closing. When and where closing is to take place, which party (buyer or seller) selects the closing agent, and who pays closing agent fees.

Title. What type of title insurance or abstract must be provided and who pays.

Assessments. Does the seller or buyer pay for assessments that are a lien?

Expiration. A date and time when the offer must be accepted before it becomes void.

Commissions. Which party owes a brokerage commission and how much it is.

Inspections. Gives buyer the right to inspect for needed repairs, structural integrity, environmental hazards, and wood-destroying insects.

City/county inspections. To ascertain compliance with local building and permit regulations.

Occupancy or operating permit. To ascertain validity.

Personal property. A list of what is included in the sale, such as furniture and equipment.

Smoke detectors. To ascertain working order and compliance with the law.

Flood plain. To advise whether the property is in a flood-prone area.

Contingency release. If the buyer must sell other property before buying this, terms of releasing buyer's rights to this contract.

Tax deferred exchange. Terms of cooperation with seller if seller desires a tax-free exchange.

Income and expense statement. To be provided by seller to buyer within a set number of days.

Existing leases. Must be delivered to buyer, as they remain binding on buyer.

Arbitration. Settlement by a specified arbitration board in the event of disputed terms.

Changes during transaction. Purchaser's consent is required for new or renegotiated rental agreements, alterations, repairs, and other matters.

Prorations. Calls for taxes, interest, insurance, or rents to be prorated between buyer and seller.

Title examination. Allows the buyer (or attorney) to examine title and submit any objections to be cleared prior to closing.

Encumbrances. Buyer is to take title subject to encumbrances, or provide, within a brief time period, objections to restrictions, easements, and unpaid taxes that must be cleared by seller.

Notices. This clause can be used to indicate that the seller, by signing the contract, is not aware of any violations of government requirements.

Default. Describes rights if a party defaults. If the buyer defaults, often the seller keeps the earnest money and may be able to collect additional amounts when the seller sustains damages. In many cases, liquidated damages are provided in the contract, and the buyer must pay them and brokerage commissions. Attorney's fees may also be paid by a defaulting buyer if a court so orders.

Physical possession. Usually allowed to buyer upon title transfer or a few days thereafter.

Time. Usually provides that time is of the essence, which prohibits delaying tactics of a party.

Other items may be put in a contract, and the wording may be arranged so that the buyer's earnest money is returned if the result does not meet expectations. For example, when buying land a rezoning may be required, or soil boring tests may be performed to determine the capability of the land to support the intended improvements. Engineering reports on structural soundness, and the absence of environmental hazards may be in the contract as contingencies.

48

NEGOTIATION

One of the keys to buying real estate is good negotiation. In the United States, prices for most products are set by the seller, but this is not the case for real estate. Consequently, participants in a real estate transaction are often unfamiliar and uncomfortable with the bargaining process. Of course, you could accept the other party's offer and complete the transaction quickly, but that would be to your financial detriment and regret.

When negotiating a price, both seller and buyer should have an idea of their *reservation prices*. This is the minimum price the seller will accept or the maximum price the buyer can pay. If you are the seller, your reservation price may be MARKET VALUE. You figure you can get this price on the market if the deal falls through. If you are the buyer, your reservation price will be INVESTMENT VALUE. This is how much the property is worth to you, considering your personal situation.

The seller will add a margin to his or her reservation price, while the buyer will subtract a margin to start the bargaining. This gives each party some bargaining room. Each hopes for better than the reservation price, if possible. Whether the seller or buyer has to come close to his or her reservation price depends on competition in the market. If there are lots of properties in the market, the buyer is in a good position and may extract concessions from the seller. If there are lots of buyers and few good properties, the seller can insist on his or her reservation price. You should be aware of the competitive condition of the market when negotiating.

Bargaining starts by the buyer making an offer for the property. The seller may accept or reject this offer, but usually comes back with a counteroffer at a higher price. The buyer then responds with another offer. The process continues until both parties agree to terms or negotiations stop due to an impasse. Often in this process of offer and counteroffer, terms of sale other than price come into play. Either party may give in on price in return for concessions on other terms. In the process, you should keep in mind your reservation price (in terms of total costs) and try to move the negotiations toward the deal that best fits your situation.

Virtually everything in a property transaction is negotiable. This means not only the price, but other terms such as:

- the form of payment (all cash at closing, deferred payments, other property);
- who pays closing costs (the seller may pay the buyer's loan discount points, title policy premium, or other costs; the buyer may pay the seller's brokerage commission);
- terms of financing, if the seller provides the loan (amount, interest rate, term of loan);
- guarantees (the seller may guarantee a minimum rental income);
- timing of closing (the buyer may wish to delay the closing to allow time to arrange financing or sign up tenants); and
- contingencies (sale subject to financing or sale of another property).

It is important to recognize that the total cost of the transaction is what counts, not merely the stated price. If you are willing to meet the seller's price, you may be able to get concessions on other items that may be more important. For example, the seller may be willing to finance the sale by lending a substantial amount of the cost. The interest rate and repayment terms then become crucial issues. Getting a lower interest rate on a long-term loan, if only 1% lower, can be equivalent to a property price reduction of up to 10%.

When negotiating, you shouldn't feel that you are trying to take advantage of the other party. Recognize that offers contain margins for bargaining and your objective is to get the best deal possible. At the same time, you must be realistic in your demands and be willing to compromise if you really want to close the deal.

49

FORECLOSED PROPERTY

There are excellent investment opportunities, but dangers, in foreclosed properties. First, you need to discover property to be considered. Then, you need to sort out the reason for foreclosure and decide whether or not you will face that same problem and, if so, whether the price is adequately discounted. Reasons for foreclosure are discussed below; sources of foreclosed properties are offered in the next Key.

Some reasons for foreclosure are:

1. **Financing,** including payments that were too high caused by:
   a. High interest rates
   b. Over-financing (too much debt)
   c. A balloon mortgage payment

2. **Rent** was too low caused by:
   a. Poor lease terms
   b. Declining rent market
   c. Poor location
   d. Declining property condition
   e. Inappropriate tenant mix
   f. Bankrupt tenant (cause of bankruptcy unrelated to the property)
   g. Loss of employment in local area

3. **Operating costs** were too high caused by:
   a. Rising taxes, insurance, utilities, maintenance and repairs
   b. No lease escalation or pass-throughs

4. **Delinquent taxes or mortgage payments** resulting from owner cash flow problems:
   a. Associated with the property
   b. Not associated with the property (related to personal problems or other property)

5. **Physical flaws**
   a. Structural: foundation cracked
   b. Costly repairs: Worn roof, leaky roof, falling fence
   c. Cosmetic repairs: Faded paint, wallpaper
   d. Shifting soil
   e. Environmental impairment: Asbestos, mold

6. **Legal**
   a. Title or ownership dispute
   b. Marital or family difficulty

Discover the reason for foreclosure by asking the current owner, prior owner, broker or salesperson, neighboring property owners or tenants; reading the newspaper or other published material; being as resourceful as possible. Don't accept the first answer, especially if it is incomplete or illogical as an explanation. Keep probing until you feel you know the real reason. Then, evaluate the property.

If the problem is a "fatal flaw," such as a serious structural defect or another problem that you will acquire with the property, drop the property from purchase consideration. If it was a financing problem, such as a high interest rate or high loan balance that you will not assume, or one that requires minor cosmetic improvements, pursue acquisition aggressively. In between are problems that are more difficult to address, such as remerchandising the space or altering the tenant mix. When the problem is due to market forces, such as rising vacancies or reduced rents, don't assume that your purchase will rejuvenate the market. Chances are that you are not the lucky charm that turns the market around.

Before entering negotiations, you should inspect the property carefully, and determine whether it is suitable for your investment purposes, just as in any other purchase. Determine your maximum price reflecting what amount will be low enough to allow rent to provide a reasonable return. Make sure your loan will be the only lien against the property. You do not want to be surprised by a bill for delinquent taxes, or other liens.

50

SOURCES OF FORECLOSED PROPERTY

Savings and loan associations, commercial banks, and credit unions make mortgage loans and Fannie Mae and Freddie Mac buy loans. When foreclosure occurs, the same institution often ends up obtaining the property to manage and resell. Commonly, they will list the property with a broker. When their inventory is unusually large, it may be worthwhile for the institution to establish an in-house management and sales staff. If a large number of properties are of the same type or are located in a limited area, the institution may hold an auction.

The Federal Housing Administration (FHA) provides insurance against default on mortgage loans. When defaults do occur, the FHA often ends up with the property following the foreclosure sale. FHA defaults are not uncommon, which means the Department of Housing and Urban Development (HUD) usually has one of the larger inventories of repossessed properties. The FHA is part of HUD.

Occasionally, HUD will place advertisements in the classified section of local newspapers. They also list properties on their web site *www.hud.gov*. Properties may include condominiums and multi-family buildings. Properties must be examined carefully, for they may be in poor condition. Don't expect a luxury home in the inventory, but you may find some good income property. Finally, HUD provides no financing, but the FHA may provide insurance on a loan you arrange with a lending institution or mortgage banker.

The Department of Veterans Affairs (VA) guarantees home loans for eligible military veterans. When a veteran defaults on the loan, the VA often buys the home in lieu of paying out the amount of the guarantee. When mortgage foreclosures have been frequent in an area, the VA is a good source of foreclosed homes.

Private mortgage insurance companies are another source. When a borrower defaults, the lender forecloses and often takes title. The lender then files a claim with the insurance company for a portion of the total losses incurred. The insurance company has the option of taking title to the property by paying the entire loan or reimbursing the lender by the amount of the claim thereby letting the lender keep the property. The oldest, and largest, is the Mortgage Guaranty Insurance Corporation (MGIC). These insurance companies may use a variety of marketing methods and have no rigid procedures for entertaining bids. You may contact the company directly for information (particularly if there have been a large number of foreclosures in the area lately), or look for ads in the paper. Many properties are higher in quality and price than those held by the FHA and VA.

The Federal Deposit Insurance Corporation (FDIC) is a government agency created to insure deposit accounts at commercial banks. When a bank fails, the FDIC moves in and obtains the assets of the failed institution (in FDIC-assisted mergers, the FDIC may take assets the merging bank does not want). These assets include any real estate owned (REO) by the failed bank.

The Federal National Mortgage Association, also referred to as "Fannie Mae" or FNMA, was created by the federal government to help organize a "secondary" market in mortgage loans. The agency uses a variety of methods to sell foreclosed property. It contracts with local brokers to list properties. It may also advertise in the local paper. Occasionally, auctions are held on a group of properties in a particular area. The Federal Home Loan Mortgage Corporation, or Freddie Mac, operates in a similar manner. Check their web sites for listings of properties for sale (*www.fanniemae .com* and *www.freddiemac.com*).

Pre-foreclosure. Foreclosure is almost always a financial catastrophe for the owner and most often presents the lender with a loss as well. Therefore, it is to everyone's interest to avoid the event. The owner will try to sell the property when facing difficulties in keeping up payments. However, if the sale will not yield enough money to pay off the loan, most financially strapped owners have little choice but to allow foreclosure to proceed.

Knowing that foreclosure sales rarely cover the outstanding loan and expenses, lenders sometimes will try to work out a solution. Such a work-out may involve restructuring the loan to provide lower monthly payments or even accepting a reduced pay-back. When a lender is willing to be flexible to revive a loan, there may be an opportunity for a third party, such as you, to forge an attractive deal. This is particularly the case when the present owner clearly has no ability or intention to retain the property. You may step into the owner's place and break the roadblock to working out a solution that avoids foreclosure.

The key to identifying such cases is a knowledgeable broker who works with owners and is aware of the possibilities of a pre-foreclosure sale. It would not be surprising if the broker has several current cases of owners faced with the difficult decision of letting their property go to foreclosure.

For additional information on the purchase of foreclosed properties, see *Keys to Buying Foreclosed and Bargain Homes*, published by Barron's Educational Series.

51

OPTION TO PURCHASE

An option is the right but not the obligation to buy. For real estate, the *option* is a right granted by the seller to a potential buyer to purchase property for a specified price within a specified period of time. It allows the buyer to keep an offer open while arranging leasing, financing, feasibility, title, easements, and zoning details. Thus, for the developer, options create LEVERAGE, reduce RISK, and conserve WORKING CAPITAL.

With an option, if you discover that the property is not as profitable as originally thought, the option is allowed to expire, and its cost is forfeited. This is far preferable to discovering problems with the property after buying.

The life of an option is generally two months to one year. The term is negotiable. Be sure it is long enough to resolve all problems that are foreseeable. In short-term options, the price is frequently fixed for the option period, whereas in longer options the purchase price may increase by steps. Sometimes the price of the option is fully credited to the purchase price of the property, and sometimes no crediting is allowed. Finally, the option may be structured so that the percentage of the option price credited against the purchase price declines with time. If buying land to be developed, the purchase of the land should be consummated only after the building permits have been obtained.

The cost of the option is negotiated but reflects: (1) the length of the option period, (2) the potential amount of appreciation in land values during the option period, (3) the possibility that another buyer will offer a higher purchase price during the option period, (4) the potential earnings that the seller will forgo by having to wait for the payment, assuming the option is executed, and (5) the seller's risk that the buyer will decide not to execute the option.

Payment for an option is different from earnest money initially paid in a typical sales contract. With the latter, the earnest money is initially paid into escrow and can be returned to the potential buyer if conditions are not met. Option money, however, is paid directly to the owner and is forfeited if the option is not exercised for any reason.

In some states, an option cannot be assigned. In other states, if you have granted the option to a certain person whom you want to perform, write a provision in the option that it cannot be assigned without your written permission. If you are acquiring the option, you will increase your flexibility if it can be sold, so you will want to include a clause allowing the assignment. A lawyer can help you ensure that nothing in the contract conflicts with state or local law.

An option can be useful anytime you want to tie up a property without taking title. Here are some situations where options are used:

Suppose you are putting together a large tract of land made up of a bunch of smaller parcels. If you can't get enough parcels to make the project work, you may want to drop the project. In that case, all you lose is your option fee.

You may need to get a property rezoned or an access road improved before you commit to buy the property. An option gives you time to arrange this. You may need to arrange construction financing for a project. An option gives you an out if the loan is not approved.

Maybe you think that some development will take place in a certain area. You can buy up options on surrounding land and speculate on higher values while limiting your risk exposure to the costs of the options.

52

DECIDING WHEN TO SELL PROPERTY

How long should investment real estate be held? Its optimal holding period varies with the property type, market conditions, and each individual investor. Perhaps the most important factor is what you'll do with the money.

Do you plan to blow the money on a new boat or reinvest it wisely? If you really just want to buy the boat, then investment strategy doesn't matter. However, as an investor considering the sale, think about the net amount you'll realize and how you'll reinvest the money. If you can't equal or exceed the return that you'll get from continuing to hold the property, keep what you have. You might consider REFINANCING, which allows you to get some money out of the property without selling it.

For example, suppose you bought a rental house a few years ago for $50,000 and now it's worth $100,000. It generates annual income of $10,000 net of operating expenses. If you sell, you'll pay a brokerage commission ($6,000), expenses of sale ($3,000), and income taxes ($11,000). You'll be left with $80,000 to reinvest. Suppose the best investment opportunity is one that yields 8%; that will provide only $6,400 annually, much less than the $10,000 you're now getting. If you can't exceed $10,000 of income on a new investment opportunity, keep the house. But if the $80,000 is needed to go into a business that promises to pay a 50% annual return, sell the house. The rate of return is like a speedometer; if your vehicle is too slow, get a faster one—if you can.

Considering a sale requires more thought than just estimating a rate of return, because it must include risk factors. The problem becomes more complex when debt is involved. As to risk, a bond may provide more safety, whereas the business venture may be much riskier than the rental house. So your personal judgment must temper a higher rate with increased risk of loss or volatility. As to financing, one must subtract the debt on property owned to determine exactly how much money will be realized from a sale. This adds more mathematics to the problem. The effect of depreciation and capital gains can add complications to the income tax estimate.

Highly leveraged real estate that appreciates in value will provide a very high yield on the equity investment. To sustain such a high yield there is a temptation to sell and buy another larger, highly leveraged property in a year or two. However, this sort of pyramiding is financially dangerous — like playing double-or-nothing. One loss and you're completely wiped out. A longer holding period tends to be safer, and you eliminate the risk associated with a new purchase.

Sometimes cash can be extracted from real estate by refinancing, thus extending the optimal holding period. Refinancing costs money but eliminates most of the expenses of a sale, including income taxes. Refinancing may provide the cash for a new boat or additional investment. But be sure you can handle the increased payments of a new loan with increased principal.

53

EXCHANGES

In most real estate investment programs, there comes a time when you need to change properties. Your property may have grown in value and now it is time to move up to a larger property. You may want to get into a different type of property, such as moving from rental housing to an office building. If you move, you may want to keep your investments close at hand. You may have several small properties and want to consolidate into one large property.

Many have found that the best way to change properties is through exchanging. They merely trade properties with another investor. This may include selling the property and reinvesting in a new one.

Another big advantage of exchanging is that you may save taxes. If your property has appreciated, you will owe taxes on CAPITAL GAINS when you sell. A 1031 exchange can let you defer paying those taxes until some time in the future. To do this, you must trade for other investment real estate (the property traded or received can't be your home). If you end up with some cash from the exchange, you may have to pay some taxes. In most cases, you will need to trade up in the exchange. If you end up with a smaller debt, you may have to pay some taxes. However, in cases where you pay some taxes, they may be less than if you sold your property for cash. There need not be an actual exchange. Section 1031 allows one to sell one's investment or business real estate and buy substitute property within certain constraints. The constraints are strict requirements of the tax law. You will likely need a qualified intermediary to assist you. This party may be called an *accommodator* or *facilitator*. The qualified intermediary should be knowledgeable of the requirements and pitfalls to avoid.

You must identify possible substitute properties within 45 days after your sale and close on the new property within 180 days of the sale. The number of properties you are allowed to identify as substitutes is limited.

You can even do exchanges with someone who doesn't have property that you want. The person you trade with can promise to find you a property to complete the trade. Taxes can still be deferred if the property is found and transferred within a certain time limit.

To exchange property, you may advertise that you want an exchange and find your own deal. Or you may find a broker who does exchanges on a regular basis. The broker may promote your property at special exchange meetings and arrange a trade among other property owners. For complicated exchanges, as when properties are not traded at the same time, it is a good idea to employ an intermediary company to handle the transaction and make sure all tax issues are resolved. Many major title insurance companies operate such firms. The rules of a tax-free exchange are described in Section 1031 of the *Internal Revenue Code*. Be sure to enlist professional tax advice when considering a trade.

For information on brokers who specialize in exchanges, see the National Council of Exchangors site (*www.nce1031.net*).

54

SELLER FINANCING

Those who sell property generally do so to raise cash to use outside the property being sold. At times, a seller may prefer or need to finance part or all of the price of property sold. The seller may take a first mortgage or a second, depending on whether there is existing assumable financing.

As compared with a cash sale, seller financing may have benefits, including spreading out the tax on the gain over the period when the principal is collected. The interest rate on the financing may greatly exceed the rate available from a bank account. However, most seller-financed loans are illiquid. The collateral is all in one property, and is illiquid. Sometimes buyers whose credit won't qualify for a bank loan seek seller financing.

Should the buyer default, it is likely that the property will have decreased in value below the mortgage(s). When the seller-financed mortgage is a first mortgage, you as seller will stop receiving mortgage payments and instead endure negative cash flows caused by legal fees and operating expenses until you can sell or rent the property. If the seller-financed loan was a second mortgage, you as seller will suffer all of the above and additionally be required to cure the default on the first mortgage and make its payments. Failure to do so will result in loss of the property. If the property seller-lender was the original borrower of the first mortgage, there may be a deficiency judgment. This occurs when the sale in foreclosure is less than the amount owed.

While a seller who provides financing may think that foreclosure would be profitable, this rarely occurs. The home purchaser will exit abruptly only when there is no equity. This may be caused by deteriorating real estate market conditions or physical deterioration of the individual property. Unless you are prepared to take the risk of again owning property that you once wanted sold, seller financing is not attractive.

Seller financing should not be provided by a real estate novice without significant assistance by a real estate attorney and a mortgage loan expert. It entails too many expensive pitfalls for the inexperienced and unwary. Help from others before entering the transaction may reduce certain risks, but not all risks of seller financing can be eliminated.

55

ZONING AND REZONING

Most cities have a zoning ordinance by which they control the use of land within their boundaries. The main purpose of *zoning* is to separate land uses that might interfere with one another. For example, most people would not want a factory or shopping center in the middle of their neighborhood. A zoning ordinance may prevent someone from building a factory in a residential area (and may prevent someone from building houses next to a factory, as well). Some cities also use zoning to try to keep development from overwhelming the capacity of roads and public services.

For a landowner, zoning means you cannot do whatever you want with your land. All land in the city is classified on a zoning map. Your land may be zoned "R2." If you look up this classification in the ordinance, it might tell you that your land is intended for up to 12 units per acre (low rise or garden apartments) and you can't build a high rise on the site. Some ordinances use *exclusive zones,* meaning you can use the land only for the uses stated for your classification. Others use *cumulative zones* where you can build anything stated in your classification or in lower density zones. For example, you may build houses in an apartment zone.

One of the keys to successful land investment is *rezoning*. The value of a well-located parcel of land can increase considerably if it is rezoned from single-family residential (worth about $10,000 per acre) to commercial use ($100,000). If you see choice property that needs to be rezoned, you might buy it using an option or a contingency clause in the contract. The clause would allow you not to complete the transaction if the land were not rezoned. In the contract you should try to allow up to a year to process a rezoning request.

When you need to change the zoning classification, you may apply to the local government. A favorable action is most successful when zoning has been changed for other parcels near yours. If the current zoning seems acceptable but a minor infraction of the ordinance is needed for a viable property use, you might apply for a *variance*. This allows you to do things that would not be allowed by strict enforcement of the ordinance.

Sometimes a property may have a building that is not allowed by the ordinance. This is called a *nonconforming* use and was probably in existence before the ordinance was written. If you have such a property, you can continue using it. You will be restricted, however, in how you modify or improve the building. Additionally, if the building is damaged, you might not be able to rebuild.

Related to, but not a part of zoning are *subdivision regulations*. These set up standards on lot size and where you can place a building on a lot. Often, the best investment in the subdivision is the house that barely meets the standards. Its value is raised by the adjacent houses that are bigger and better. Usually there are *setback* requirements, meaning you can't put a building too close to the front or sides of the lot. These regulations may also require you to hook up to city water and sewer systems. Be wary of expensive requirements for hookups and for moratoriums on hooking up. These can make what seems like a surefire investment turn into a frustrating loser.

Zoning should not be confused with *condemnation*. When the government needs your land for some public project, such as a new road or urban renewal clearance, it can force you to sell for appraised value. (When your land is restricted under zoning, the government need not compensate you for any loss in value. Sometimes land adjacent to the condemnation can skyrocket in value.) Try to buy next to the highway interchange—rural land bought this way can turn into commercial property in an instant.

In addition to zoning, your land may be restricted by private *deed covenants*. These are part of the contract you signed when you bought the property. Such covenants may affect the design of any building put on the land and may prevent you from using the land for certain purposes.

56

BUILDING AND
HOUSING CODES

Cities often set up standards for construction called *building codes;* for maintenance, they are called *housing codes*. In addition, there may be various health codes which affect restaurants and hotels. These local codes are intended to prevent unsafe conditions in buildings and protect the general public. An important federal law is the Americans with Disabilities Act (ADA), intended to protect the handicapped.

If you are building a structure or making repairs or improvements to your property, you may need to get a *building permit*. You will pay a nominal fee and agree to have the work inspected by a city official. The building code describes certain types of materials and design standards that must be used. There are usually separate codes for the structure, plumbing, electrical, and heating systems. For some tasks, you may be required to hire a licensed contractor to comply with the code. After you pass the inspection, you are issued a *certificate of occupancy* meaning the building is fit to be used by the public.

Housing codes set standards for the maintenance of residential buildings. These are usually minimum standards relating to conditions where the building might collapse or encourage pests and disease. If your building is found in violation of the code, it may be condemned by the city and you won't be allowed to use it or rent it out.

When buying property, it is important to inspect it for code violations. If it is new construction, make sure it has passed all required inspections. If it is old property, see that it passes the housing code (unless you intend to redevelop the property). All violations are the responsibility of the owner and you may face unexpected repairs if you don't take precautions.

The ADA was aimed at freeing some 43 million Americans from discrimination by requiring the removal of barriers to the handicapped. Cost of barrier removal may affect an investor's decision to purchase property, or at least the price one is willing to pay, so knowledge of costs should be incorporated into a purchaser's offer by reducing the offer if faced with substantial amounts to comply.

The ADA requires owners and tenants of "places of public accommodation" to modify practices that discriminate against the disabled, provide auxiliary aids to communication, and remove architectural barriers (if removal can be "readily achieved" and does not constitute an "undue burden").

Public places affected include ones that are public and privately owned. A sample includes:

1. Hotels and motels
2. Restaurants and bars
3. Theaters, stadiums, and concert halls
4. Auditoriums, convention centers, lecture halls
5. Sales or rental establishments such as shopping centers, grocery stores
6. Service establishments such as banks, laundromats, gas stations, funeral parlors
7. Airport, bus terminals
8. Museums, libraries
9. Schools, parks

Some examples of barrier removal are:

1. Installing ramps
2. Making curb cuts in sidewalks and entrances
3. Repositioning shelves
4. Installing a raised toilet seat, grab-bars in toilet stalls, rearranging partitions to increase maneuvering space

Housing needs of the handicapped are protected by the Federal Fair Housing Amendment Act of 1988. This law made it illegal to discriminate against the handicapped in housing. Accordingly, a landlord must lease to a blind tenant needing a seeing eye dog, even if dogs are otherwise prohibited in the apartments.

This law also protects families from housing discrimination. For example, single parent households must be served, and adults-only apartment complexes are no longer allowed unless they serve the elderly almost exclusively.

57

ENVIRONMENTAL CONSIDERATIONS

Increased environmental sensitivity has raised the liability of those involved in real estate. Every gas station could have a leaking tank, pump, or pipe that contaminates ground water. Dry cleaners and car washes may use chemicals that, if released, are harmful. Even seemingly innocent property uses such as golf courses and agricultural land are suspect because of fertilizer and pesticide applications. A typical real estate insurance policy will not provide for repairs caused by environmental impairment.

A property may host radon, have lead-based paint, have had pesticides liberally applied to the lawn, have urea formaldehyde or asbestos insulation, or host black mold. It may be near a landfill, or have been built on contaminated land. Due diligence for the investigation of homes that would require an inspection of records of prior ownership and land use and an inspection of the property is suggested.

Liability. *Superfund* is the common name for the 1980 law that affects many issues of real estate contamination. Superfund, reauthorized in 1986 as SARA, includes stronger cleanup standards, disclosure requirements, and funding.

Superfund requires the clean up, but Superfund pays only in extreme situations, and it can render property worthless. It imposes liability on those involved with hazardous materials; liability that is *strict, joint* and *several,* and *retroactive.*

Liability is created by Superfund in any connection with the property: as an owner, operator, generator, or transporter. *Strict* means that it doesn't matter whether such a person acted knowingly or reasonably—that person bears liability. The absence of negligence or other wrongdoing is not a defense. There are some legal defenses but they are limited.

Joint and several liability means that every responsible party is liable for the full cost. The government or Superfund claimant may find anyone with a "deep pocket" to pay costs, and doesn't have to sort out who was responsible for how much damage. Huge cleanup costs could conceivably be assessed against someone who took title for an instant during a closing to facilitate a transaction, but otherwise had no involvement with the property. The unlucky party would be responsible for the full amount, but could seek reimbursement from other responsible parties.

Retroactive liability means that it reaches back to prior owners and operators. This overrides "as is" clauses in sales contracts. It also precedes any mortgage lien.

Activities. Activities that may cause contamination include manufacturing, assembly, repair, laboratory, storage, machine shop services, and cleaning. A partial list of types of businesses that may be perpetrators include any that use, manufacture, or supply products to these users: electronics, leathers, paints, pesticides, petroleum, pharmaceuticals, plastics, refining, smelting, or textiles. In addition to those activities, events that may cause serious problems include fires, explosions, spills, and tank, pump, and pipe leaks.

Contaminated Items. Contamination can be found in buildings, soil, and groundwater. Within a building, asbestos may have been used for insulation and pipe-wrapping. There is no problem unless the asbestos is friable, which means it crumbles. Interior components of a building may have thick residues of chemicals that were used—these may have migrated through concrete floors into the soil.

Underground petroleum storage tanks (USTs) may leak. This is a common problem. To determine if there is a known leaking petroleum storage tank (LPST) nearby, contact the appropriate state agency. Many state agencies have web sites, and can tell you the degree of contamination and the status of the clean-up, i.e., just reported or case closed. It is important to determine whether there is a party who is monitoring the level of contamination and is responsible for the clean-up.

Contamination that spreads through groundwater can cause problems to adjacent property. An extensive site assessment might be needed to determine the extent of damage.

If the state agency that monitors LPSTs has issued a "no further action is required" or "closure" letter, there should be no problem with the site or adjacent property. Typically, these parcels can be sold or financed without a problem.

Black mold may be found in any type of property but tends to flourish near moist, poorly ventilated places. Sometimes it may be growing between walls and therefore difficult to find. Black mold is not just unsightly—it is a health hazard that, in a worst case, may render property worthless.

Detection. A proper site assessment by a qualified professional is the best approach when considering a purchase. More and more lenders are requiring one as a requisite for a mortgage loan on commercial or industrial property, as contaminants can render a property worthless, and a foreclosure makes the lender an owner who is liable. Site assessment costs range from a few thousand to hundreds of thousands, and include drilling tests, electrical conducting, ground penetration, and laboratory analysis. An aerial photograph may help identify suspect points.

Other methods of due diligence to determine detection include reviewing public records and newspapers and checking with the local fire department and state or federal environmental or pollution agencies. A Phase I assessment should be performed by a buyer as part of the due diligence acquisition process; it will help avoid clean up liability under Superfund. Phase II estimates the cost of clean up, and Phase III performs the work.

Disclosure. The Environmental Protection Agency (EPA) requires the seller to disclose knowledge of the existence of lead based paint in houses built before 1988, and may require written notice of a renovation or remodeling that occurred prior to 1988.

QUESTIONS AND ANSWERS

As an investment, does real estate have any advantages over other types of assets?

The main difference between real property and assets like stocks and bonds is that real estate not only can provide a regular income, but its value tends to keep up with inflation. Therefore, real estate can be a good investment when inflation is a concern. In fact, many real estate investors try to find properties that can appreciate at a rate greater than inflation. This can boost investment return greatly.

It is relatively easy to arrange financing for real estate purchases. This gives you the advantages of LEVERAGE. Your return may be magnified because you can keep any income after paying debt service on the loan. This is like buying stock on margin.

If you buy property directly, you have control over its operation. You decide on tenants, maintenance, remodeling, and when to sell. You may find properties that can be improved through renovation or conversion. This can add to your return.

Real estate provides some tax advantages. Depreciation may be deducted from rental income on a tax return. This allows some, perhaps all, of the cash flow to be received tax free. If you own the property directly and make your own management decisions, you may be allowed to use negative taxable income from the property to offset other income, thus paying less tax on income earned outside the property. In addition, if you sell business real estate for a loss, you can claim the entire loss in the year of sale, rather than using only $3,000 of capital loss as with stocks or bonds.

Of course, real estate can be purchased through a partnership or by shares in a real estate investment trust. These forms allow you to spread your capital over many properties and relieve you of management responsibilities. They also make it easier to get into and out of an investment.

How about disadvantages?

Real estate is expensive. Even when using borrowed money, purchase of a property requires a sizable investment of cash. This makes it hard to spread your investment among several properties. However, you can invest through partnerships to get more diversification.

The success of a real estate investment depends on many factors that you can't control. The local economy determines how much trouble you will have finding tenants and getting rents sufficient to cover expenses. Local builders can flood the market with similar projects, giving you extra competition that may not have been expected. Government regulations can affect how you operate your property and restrict any changes you may want to make. Remember, if you are having trouble in your present location, you can't move the property to another place.

Although the use of borrowed money is an advantage of real estate, leverage also increases the risk of failure. A loss in rental income may leave you with insufficient net operating income to make your debt payments. If you can't afford to make up the difference, you may lose the property through foreclosure. A downturn in market value can wipe out any equity (the portion of value over the loan balance) in the property. If you are forced to sell during such a downturn, you may lose your invested capital.

Property you own directly requires management. Someone must oversee operations and upkeep. This may require constant contact with tenants, maintenance people, and repairmen. If the property is big enough, you can arrange for a property manager to do these tasks. You can also hire a real estate broker to find tenants and collect rent for you. However, use of professionals involves costs that must come out of your return.

Lastly, property is not always easy to sell. The transactions are complicated and can be costly. You often may find that buyers are hard to locate. You can't easily convert your investment into cash, especially if you want a good return. You should have emergency cash reserves put away outside of your real estate investments.

Who should be a real estate investor?

Most people are real estate investors perhaps without realizing it. They have purchased a home that represents a good portion of their personal wealth. So your first real estate decision is whether to buy a home. Home ownership can be a good deal financially. You may fix a major portion of your housing expense without worrying about rent increases, find a large proportion of your expenses (interest and property taxes) are tax deductible, and realize some profit when it is time to sell. However, the money you put into a home may be hard to recover if you need it in an emergency. While you own the home, you are responsible for anything that goes wrong. When you sell, you are at the mercy of market conditions.

These same factors come into play with real estate investments other than your home. Therefore, you must decide if your personal situation fits with real estate ownership. You should be familiar with the local area to judge the value of particular locations. You should have sufficient cash to make a purchase and cover periodic expenses without depleting money set aside for emergencies. You should not put yourself in a situation where you must sell at a profit within a certain amount of time. You should be able and willing to take care of the property and respond to tenants' problems as needed.

Today, real estate investment is flexible enough to fit many investor situations. If you desire periodic income, you can invest in conservative properties with good cash flow. If you want growth, you can speculate in undeveloped land or properties with conversion potential. If you don't want management responsibilities or unlimited risk, you can buy into a limited partnership. If you want an investment that is easy to buy and sell, you can buy shares of a REIT. To some extent, you can tailor your involvement to your situation.

What should an investor look for in a property?

The main concern for a real estate investor should be the ability of a property to hold its value. Appreciation can be a source of high returns, but a loss in value may wipe out your investment. One key is to know what the property is worth on the market. You can get this information by ordering a market value appraisal. This will help guard against paying too much for the property, recognizing that seller offering prices are generally overstated.

Look for a location that works well with the intended use of the property. Don't buy an office building with poor parking or an apartment building in a neighborhood with rising crime. Try to picture where development is moving and buy ahead of the movement.

Unless you intend to renovate or redevelop the property, have it inspected for physical problems. You don't want surprises after you buy the property. Often you can find property that just needs some paint and minor repairs to greatly improve its value.

If the property is occupied, check the current leases and tenants. Some may not be paying rent or rents may be far below market levels. Once you step in, these tenants may disappear. If leases are long-term, you may not be able to increase rents in line with expenses.

Can I save taxes by investing in real estate?

Income tax benefits have been a traditional attraction to real estate. In 1986, Congress tried to reduce this attraction and make real estate more like other investments. However, there are still some advantages. The major one comes from deductions for depreciation. You can deduct a portion of the value of man-made parts of the property each year from the property's income. This makes some of the cash flow you receive from the property tax-free. If your deductions exceed income from the property, you can apply the difference to other income, assuming you own the property directly and meet other requirements.

Profits from resale may be taxed at favorable capital gains rates. Long-term capital gains to individuals are generally taxed at a 15% maximum, though the capital gains rate may be 5% or less. A higher but still favorable rate is applied to long-term gains attributable to certain prior real estate depreciation claimed. You may have property that is appreciating in value, but you don't pay taxes on the appreciation until you sell. If you exchange the property for other real estate, you may be able to defer payment of taxes on any increased value. If you sell for a loss, real estate used in a trade or business, you can deduct the full amount of the loss in the year of sale.

Under present law, unrealized appreciation escapes income taxes at death. The property value at death is subject to estate taxation.

What makes real estate go up and down in value?

Real estate markets tend to be cyclical. This means that demand tends to rise at times to exceed the supply and at other times to fall below the amount of property available. This creates periods of seller's markets—with prices rising—and periods of buyer's markets—characterized by falling prices.

There are well-known factors that stimulate the demand for real property (the demand from users of the

172

space and the investor demand to purchase buildings are different economically but related to one another). Rising employment and economic prosperity create demand for all types of real property, from homes to warehouses. Easing credit and low interest rates trigger the demand for homes. As we saw in 2008, however, the withdrawal of credit can have dire effects on housing demand and property values.

Because real property is long-lived and immobile, supply is relatively slow to change, so fluctuations in demand can cause wide swings in prices. Also, it takes time to increase supply, and new buildings sometimes come to market after demand has shifted direction, leading to surpluses and lower prices.

The investment attraction of real property complicates the cycle of supply and demand. Speculative markets are created by expectations that prices will continue to climb unabated. Prices are bid upward until that confidence is broken.

How can I control risk when investing?

Risk can never be totally eliminated in any investment, but it can be limited. By performing some type of analysis of the investment, you have some idea how risky it is. Investment analysis shows you the type of return you can expect and how much that return depends on maintaining cash flow or getting a good resale price. An investment that depends on maintaining a proven level of cash flow is less risky than one that depends on value appreciation. Also, an investment that uses a lot of LEVERAGE is more risky than one with a modest amount of debt financing.

Some risk can be reduced by buying insurance. Most property owners use insurance to guard against physical damage due to accidents or hazards. These policies also cover liability of someone getting hurt on the property.

If you own property directly, either alone or with a partner, your risk extends beyond the property. If the property runs into trouble and the loan is foreclosed, the lender may look to any other property you own to make up any deficiency. However, you may insulate yourself from such risk by changing the way you own the property. You may set up a corporation, an LLC, or S Corporation to own the property. Only the resources of the corporation can be used to backup the loan. Another way is to buy into a limited partnership. In this case, you are risking only the money invested in the partnership.

Buying shares of a REIT or a real estate mutual fund provides diversification for even the small investor. This makes the results less dependent on one property or location.

Risk can also be limited by getting a nonrecourse loan. The lender agrees that the property will be the sole security for the debt. Expect the lender to require some concession, such as a higher interest rate, for the nonrecourse provision.

What is the best way to invest in real estate?

There is no best way, but there may be a way that is best suited to your situation. It depends on how closely you want to be involved with a property.

You can buy property directly. A real estate broker can show you investment properties currently on the market. Many investors start out buying single-family homes and renting them out. These are often the least expensive alternatives and the easiest to understand for the beginning investor. Another strategy is to buy a duplex. This offers the opportunity to live in part of the property while renting out the rest. Direct ownership gives you maximum control of the property but also all the responsibility. You can hire someone to take care of overseeing the property and a real estate broker to find tenants and collect rent.

If you want a more passive role, there are several alternatives to invest in real estate. Professional investors, called *syndicators,* set up limited partnerships to buy property. In many cases, you can buy into a partnership for a cash investment of a few thousand dollars.

The syndicator manages the property and you have a limited role in its operation. When the property is sold, the partnership is dissolved. Some large partnerships own many properties, which helps spread the risk that any one property will run into trouble. Syndicated partnerships often require high fees so only a portion of your money goes into the property. Also a partnership interest may be difficult to transfer if you want to get your money out.

A *real estate investment trust* (REIT) allows you to buy shares of stock that can be easily sold in the market. The trust owns property (some lend money to others to buy property) and passes almost all of the income from the properties to shareholders. If you own shares in a REIT, you probably won't even know what properties are owned, but you may get your money out at any time by selling the shares. Like stock shares, of course, the value of the REIT shares may change over time.

What types of studies are done on real estate and how can they help me make decisions?

Because each property is unique, individual analyses must be performed to indicate its value and investment potential. There are several types of studies performed by trained professionals that are commonly used.

An *appraisal* gives you an indication of what the property is worth. Most appraisals indicate market value or the amount of money a buyer would likely pay for the property under normal conditions. Appraisals can also tell you how much the buildings are worth as apart from the land, how much it would cost to reproduce the building today, what similar properties have sold for recently, and rent levels for other properties in the market.

A *market analysis* tells you what the demand for the property is. It identifies the type of tenants or buyers the property will attract and how many there are. It also gives an idea of the competition that is vying for those same tenants. Market analysis is generally used in the early stages of a proposed project to determine what type of development should be considered.

A *feasibility study* carries market analysis further to indicate whether a development should be considered. It attempts to project the likely success of the development and whether you will get the type of return you want.

More generally, *investment analysis* looks at any type of investment, whether new construction or existing property. It projects future revenues and expenses to estimate cash flow and return on invested cash. The analysis may be a simple one-year projection or may cover the entire period you expect to own the property. The result is some type of return indicator, such as a cash-on-cash return or internal rate of return. These indicators can be used to compare other opportunities to invest your money. Some type of investment analysis, even a simple one, is recommended before you commit to a purchase.

Why is financing so important?

Few investors have enough cash to purchase or develop a property without financing. Even if you do have enough cash, you may not want to put it all into one property. Therefore, getting a loan is just about essential if you want to own real estate.

When you use financing, you get LEVERAGE. This means that any return from the property is magnified for the cash you invest. This is because your loan payments are usually fixed and don't depend on the success of the property. Anything left after you make the loan payment and meet expenses is yours. If you made a small down payment and the property produces a good cash flow, your rate of return is much larger than if you had paid all cash. On the other hand, if the property doesn't produce enough rent to pay operating expenses and loan payments, you will have to make up the difference from other income. This is why you should be careful not to use so much financing that you are constantly struggling to make ends meet.

The terms under which you get financing can make or break your investment. When interest rates are high, it may be impossible to get a loan that doesn't take all of the net operating income in loan payments. In such cases, sellers often make a loan to the buyer at a rate that is attractive. Such loans generally have balloon payments (equal to the balance of the loan) due after a few years. When the balloon is due, you must refinance. If interest rates are still high, you may have difficulty keeping the property.

What is the best source for a real estate loan?

The best source is where you can get the best terms. You will want to get a loan that is large enough to allow purchase of the property you want, but at a reasonable interest rate. If you think rates are going up, you will want a long-term, fixed-rate loan, preferably with a provision to allow a buyer to assume the loan. If rates look like they are going down, you may want a short-term loan or an adjustable-rate loan.

A common source of real estate loans are institutional lenders. Commercial banks generally make short-term loans but may offer longer terms on real estate. Savings and loan (S&L) associations specialize in real estate loans, particularly housing. Banks and S&Ls usually hold the loans they make. Mortgage bankers offer loans that they sell to investors or in the secondary mortgage market. The loans they make are those that are desired in these markets, mainly on residential properties.

It is not uncommon for sellers to provide financing. In some cases, you may assume the existing loan from the seller. This loan may carry an attractive rate of interest but may require a large amount of cash to make up the difference between the loan amount and the sales price. The seller may make a new loan by taking back a note as partial payment for the property. The seller loan may be in addition to a loan assumption or the primary debt on the property. Seller loans are usually short term but at rates below the current market. Terms on the seller loan are negotiated along with the sales price.

What is an operating statement?

An *operating statement* shows the cash flow from a property. You will have to put one of these together each year to report taxable income. When you apply for a loan to purchase or refinance a property, you will need to construct a statement for the next year. This is called a *pro-forma statement* because it is a projection of cash flow for the year.

A sample real estate operating statement in its standard form might be:

Potential gross income	$ 110,000
Vacancy and collection allowance	– 5,000
Miscellaneous income	+ 5,000
Effective gross income	$ 110,000
Operating expenses	– 45,000
Net operating income	$ 65,000
Debt service	– 50,000
Before-tax cash flow	$ 15,000
Income tax attributable to property income	– 2,000
After-tax cash flow	$ 13,000

Potential gross income is the amount that would be collected in rents if the property were fully occupied. Vacancy and collection allowance is rental income lost from vacant units and rents that could not be collected from tenants. Miscellaneous income is from nonrental sources, such as concessions, parking fees, or advertising fees. *Effective gross income* is the total revenues actually collected. *Operating expenses* are outlays for management, maintenance, repairs, utilities, property taxes, and insurance.

Net operating income is what the property produced. From this amount, loan payments and taxes must be paid. *Debt service* is the total paid for the year in principal and interest on the loan. Taxes are calculated from net operating income less depreciation and interest payments. Taxes are usually based on your marginal tax rate, or the highest tax bracket your income falls into. *Cash flow* is what you keep and can be expressed as a before- or after-tax amount.

What are the most important things to know when signing up tenants?

Before looking for tenants, you must decide on what type of lease provisions you want. Much of this will be determined by your competition. You will want a rental rate that provides a reasonable cash flow but is not out of line with other similar properties. Will you pay some of the utilities? Most owners avoid utility payments unless the rental units are not separately metered. If a commercial building is leased to a single tenant, the tenant is often responsible for upkeep and maintenance. If you want this provision, you must prepare a net lease.

How long should the lease term be? A long lease gives you more security and reduces tenant search efforts, but increases the risk that expenses will rise more than rental income. You may want to include cost-of-living increases in the lease when the term is for several years.

In selecting tenants, you want to know that they can afford to pay the rent and will not destroy the property. You may require references from previous landlords and operating statements from business tenants. You should be concerned that your tenants will not interfere with each other's use of the property. This may mean separating adults from couples with small children within an apartment complex. (In residential properties, keep in mind that your selection of tenants is governed by open housing laws that outlaw racial, age, and sex discrimination.) In shopping centers, tenants will not want to locate close to competing businesses. In many cases, anchor tenants, much larger than the other stores in the complex, are necessary to get financing.

What types of expenses can I expect when operating a rental property?

The costs involved with operation of a property are called *operating expenses*. They fall into several standard categories. Some of these are fixed, in that they do not vary with occupancy. You are required to pay property taxes to the local government. This tax is based on the market value of your property and may vary from less than 1% up to over 4% of value, depending on where the property is. You will need to carry insurance against damage and liability as a minimum. Premiums depend on the replacement cost of the building, the policy's coinsurance level, and the risk of hazard or liability claims calculated by the insurance company. Expect the premium to run from .5% to 1% percent of property value.

Variable expenses depend on the occupancy of the building. You may have some type of utility payments, either in the building if your tenants do not pay their own utilities, or to light and heat common areas. You may have to hire someone to clean the building, do lawn chores, and tend to other things necessary to keep the property presentable. You can manage the property yourself or hire someone to take care of it. If you hire a manager, the fee is generally a percentage of the rental income collected. You should expect some expenses for repair and replacement of building parts, such as plumbing fixtures, carpeting, window glass, and other breakable or short-lived items. You may want to keep a reserve for these expenses. Finally, there are many *miscellaneous expenses,* such as office supplies, advertising, fees, and payroll taxes you pay for any employees you hire.

How do I know when to sell a property?

There comes a time when you must change investments to achieve your long-range investment program. The property you have may have been profitable and increased in value. You may want to move up to a larger property with more LEVERAGE. On the other hand, the property may not have turned out so well. It may be time to take your loss and try another type of property. Or it could be that you are tired of operating the property and want something different.

A key to making the decision to sell is considering how you will invest the proceeds from a sale. A strong market for properties may tempt you to sell, but remember that you must reinvest in that same market. In such a market, you may consider refinancing the loan and keeping the property. By doing this you increase leverage while keeping a known property. The money from the refinancing may be used to buy other investments. Another strategy is to sell and take profits, then invest the proceeds in stocks or bonds until you can find a bargain property.

One problem with selling a property that has appreciated is the taxes you must pay on the gain. The increase in value and all prior depreciation claimed becomes taxed when you sell. If you want to stay in real estate, but want to change properties, you may consider an exchange. If you exchange for real estate, you can defer taxes on the gain. The money you would have used for taxes can be invested in the new property.

If your property has been disappointing, and the prospects for improvement don't look promising, it may be time to change. Any loss taken on the sale can be used to reduce taxes on your other income.

When I sell, should I use a real estate broker?

Real estate brokers are in the market constantly and are knowledgeable about market conditions. They can advise you on setting an offering price, contact potential buyers, present the property, and help set up the negotiations needed to get a sales contract. For these services, brokers charge a commission equal to some percentage of the selling price. You pay a commission only if the broker is successful in finding a willing buyer for your property.

Some property owners try to sell their properties without using a broker. If successful, they save themselves the commission fee. If you should decide to take this route, be prepared to advertise the property and spend time with prospective buyers. If the market is not active, this process may take many months. You should also know something about setting up real estate sales contracts to assist the buyer in the transaction.

Most "for sale by owner" properties are homes. Marketing an investment property without a broker is much more rare. A good commercial property broker has contacts with investors and knows how to prepare presentations that show the investment benefits of the property. In addition, the broker may be able to advise you on different ways to package your property.

The recent housing bust is considered the end of a "bubble." What is a bubble in the context of a market?

Markets, including real estate markets, go through cycles of rising and falling prices. These cycles are usually based on changes in underlying supply and demand conditions or the investment outlook. Sometimes, however, an upward run in prices can feed on itself and send prices spiraling ever upward. This market is likened to a bubble because property values inflate beyond all reason and eventually reach a level that cannot be sustained. That is when the bubble bursts, leading to a relentless and rapid downward slide. Investors who bought property at or near the top of the market often lose most or all of their investment. A total loss of equity and more may inure to real estate investors who leveraged (borrowed) against their purchase.

What causes these bubbles?

Current property selling prices are based largely on psychological expectations of future price increases. When a market is on a bull run (an upward trend), with demand strong and prices rising consistently, expectations can be so stimulated as to drive up prices further. A strong upward price run also tends to weed out the naysayers and build a consensus among participants of the inevitability of higher prices. In extreme cases, expectations take on a life of their own, leading market participants to ignore fundamentals as a basis for pricing. Purchases become speculations, and prudent investors and owner-tenants no longer dominate the market. Speculators dominate.

Isn't a bubble just part of the normal real estate cycle?

Real estate markets are reasonably efficient (market prices reflect all that is known about a property), though with a time lag. When demand changes unexpectedly, it may take a year or longer before new supply is produced and decades before an excess supply of buildings will be retired. As a result, periods of oversupply and undersupply occur regularly. An oversupply is characterized by high vacancy rates and falling rents. By contrast, undersupply shows up in rapidly rising rental rates and very tight supply. When supply falls short of demand, prices naturally go up. When this persists for a while, expectations of further price rises become more intense and extensive. When almost everyone thinks that prices will rise further, conditions are ripe for a bubble. Unlike normal cycles, however, bubbles are based on an exaggeration and misreading of demand, confusing purchases by speculators with genuine demand for use of the property.

How could a housing bubble continue for such a long time?

The housing boom of the early 2000s survived a slowdown in economic activity following the dot-com bust that would normally dissipate all speculative activity in the market. There were several reasons for this that were peculiar to the time.

First, with the stock market retreating in 2000–2002, housing was one of the few places to make money. Indeed, the yields on mortgage securities really looked good in the light of low interest rates and falling stock prices.

Second, the mortgage market was expanding to an unprecedented degree. People who would never previously have been considered for a mortgage were able to get loans with little or no money down. The high yields on "subprime" loans encouraged their expansion, and the new methodology of credit scoring promised to weed out potential defaulters much more effectively than the largely subjective methods used previously. The federal government boosted this expansion of credit in the pursuit of higher levels of homeownership and used the government-sponsored agencies Fannie Mae and Freddie Mac to implement these policies.

Finally, financial innovations allowed capital to flow to mortgages from many parts of the financial arena and created a false sense of security because of their complexity. These elements all tended to artificially increase demand and weakened the linkage to market fundamentals. However, that link returned when the underlying market collapsed.

Is it inevitable that the bubble will burst?

When a market enters a bubble, fundamental-based demand tends to tail off as prices soar. Prudent investors and those buying for their own use tend to drop out, leaving the market to speculators—those buying in hopes of a quick turnover and profit. Each buyer expects to achieve the run-up in value that the last owner received. Indeed, speculators can keep these prices high by bidding among themselves. However, as some owners cash in, expectations of rising prices or even the appearance of a greater fool cause the market to become more fragile. A property may sit on the market too long. Another property sells only after a significant price reduction. Maybe another is sold after the owner resorts to providing special financing or some other concession.

Soon, property owners adjust their psychological expectations downward. Because so much of the price is based on expectations, it becomes apparent that property prices are unrealistically high. And because prices initially are "sticky" on the downside, a bubble market may go into a state of shock after it bursts. A true bubble market sends prices way above those justified by current incomes of potential users and credible rental rates. Asking prices may have a long downward slide before any prudent investors show interest. Some property owners go into denial because they are reluctant to realize big losses, and some have problems with high amounts of mortgage debt, so they try to hold out for another greater fool. A round of foreclosures may be required to eventually clear the market. The bubble markets of the 1980s required a bailout of lending institutions before properties found their way back on the non-government market at justifiable valuations.

What market signals indicate that a bubble is topping out?

- *Real estate becomes a hot investment topic.* Everybody has an opinion on the market. There is a well-known story about Bernard Baruch, the legendary investor. One day in 1929, he received an unsolicited stock tip from the kid who shined his shoes. When he got to his office he sold everything he had in the stock market. To him, the fact that the least financially knowledgeable people felt they had a handle on the market was a sure sign that prices had gotten out of hand. The same thing may be true of real estate markets when average people get enthusiastic about buying and selling properties.

- *Investors do not seem to care about the income generated by the property.* The expectation is that appreciation gains are sufficient to make holding the property worthwhile. During the 1980s Oil Patch Bubble, developers, aided by lenders, erected "see-through" buildings—retail, office, apartments—with no tenants in hand. They thought that appreciation and tax shelter provided more than enough incentive to begin the construction process.
- *Unusual financing becomes widely available.* Such methods as interest-only loans, seller financing, and investor participations become the way to buy property. There is nothing inherently wrong with these methods when used to overcome special problems. Beware when they become the mainstream because it means that sellers are resorting to unorthodox methods to keep demand in play.
- *Highly publicized seminars on making huge profits in real estate proliferate.* Market bubbles are the heyday for the "no money down" advocates and those hyping techniques to ordinary people lured in by the expectation of making a fortune in real estate with little background or knowledge of real estate markets or property management.
- *Lots of reasons are offered for why this market cycle is different from the past.* Interest rates are low and falling (and will always be low and falling), all other investment media are performing badly (and will never turn around), real estate is specially advantaged (and will continue to be) by inflation, which will bail out any purchase. These and other claims of this sort are brought out whenever anyone questions the sustainability of the rally.
- *New housing units far exceed the number of new jobs created in an area.* Normally, local job growth fuels population inflow, which generates housing demand. When local employment is rising slowly or not at all, and new housing units are being created,

an oversupply of housing can be expected. However, new employment will not be a good test in retirement or vacation communities.

- *Ownership costs far exceed rental rates.*

What indicators let investors know that a market is bottoming out?

- *Real estate is considered a dangerous asset to own.* Anything attached to real property is a "toxic asset" in this atmosphere. People only remember how much has been lost by speculators who were left holding property when the market turned downward.
- *Mortgage foreclosures dominate the news.* You will be constantly reminded of the escalating number of loans in foreclosure and the number of homes being repossessed by lenders. A few celebrity victims of foreclosure will make the news reports. Also expect stories about banks struggling with bad loans.
- *Mortgage financing is hard to get.* Lenders burned by rising loan defaults and pressed to maintain capital reserve requirements close up shop for all but the most creditworthy. Minimum down payments increase as well as the minimum credit score needed for the most favorable terms. Despite lower prices, many would-be homebuyers are shut out of the market because of new loan standards.
- *Home prices fall without stimulating more sales.* Normally, a drop in price is accompanied by an increase in sales. In a down housing market, however, that may not be the case. Part of the reason is the tighter supply of mortgage finance that restricts the number of buyers who can qualify to buy. Another part is the need for the market to dissipate the price premium built up during the speculative spiral. Demand may not be stimulated until prices become more reasonable in relation to personal income.

- *More single-family homes become rental homes.* Many homeowners who have bought a new home find they cannot sell their old house and will turn to renting it out to generate some income.
- *Builders face bankruptcy.* Homebuilders, who could not keep up with demand during the bubble, are now left with a large unsold inventory. Some will go out of business, and some will consolidate through merger.

Can I make money buying and selling foreclosed homes?

A "foreclosed" home is one in which the holder of the mortgage on the home has taken action to cure a default on the loan used to finance purchase of the home. In other words, the homeowner has failed to live up to the loan agreement (make timely payments) and the lender is trying to get control of the house so as to pay off the debt.

Usually there is a period of time between when the lender notifies the homeowner of the problem and the actual takeover of the property. That is one opportunity for an investor to step in. A pre-foreclosure sale might be arranged where the investor becomes the owner and the homeowner escapes with credit rating unscathed. A "short sale" might even be arranged at a price below the existing debt level. If the lender (or often the entity that insured or guaranteed the loan) has already acquired the property, the investor might try to buy the "REO" from the lender, often through auction.

The key to making money from any of these transactions is to limit the amount you have to spend to acquire the home, prepare it for resale, and sell it. You will need to evaluate the property to figure out how much to bid and how much will be needed to make it attractive in the market. You will also need some legal help to make sure the deed you receive is marketable and that you are not taking on legal liabilities not apparent on the surface (such as environmental problems). If you can solve these problems, you can make money from such opportunities, but they are not for the uninitiated.

In general, unless a property has immediate potential for some other use or can be improved substantially, its value should be grounded by the income it produces. Therefore, capitalizing this income should provide a good indication of what it is worth. If you do a discounted cash flow analysis (*see* DISCOUNTED CASH FLOW TECHNIQUES/15), be careful of the growth rate you assume for rentals and property value. One way to check the rate for reasonableness is to calculate the cap rate at the projected resale date.

How can I check the consistency of my assumptions of value appreciation with growth in net operating income?

You can do this by determining the change in capitalization rates. Here's how:

- Project out the sales price you would get if your assumed rate of appreciation holds. Let's say you can buy the property for $250,000, plan to hold it for 10 years, and assume it will go up in value by 10% each year. The assumed resale price will be $648,436 after ten years.
- Project out the net operating income at the assumed rate of growth you applied to rents and operating expenses. Let's say you project rents and expenses to grow by 5% per year. When you purchase the property, effective rent is $40,000 and operating expenses are $25,000, leaving annual net operating income of $15,000. Your assumed growth rates would yield a rent of $65,156 and expenses of $40,722 at the time of resale. Thus you expect your net operating income to go from $15,000 to $24,434 while you own the property.
- Calculate the cap rate based on your purchase price and at the time of resale. At purchase the cap rate is

$15,000 divided by $250,000 or 6%. The rate under the projected terms at resale is $24,434 divided by $648,436 or 3.77%. Can such a reduction in cap rates be justified?

- Analyze what economic forces might improve to make the cap rate change. Do you expect interest rates to fall or the resale conditions to improve to justify a lower cap rate? (Remember that the lower the cap rate, the more the amount of money investors are willing to pay for the same income stream.) Most of the time at market peaks, the outlook and market conditions are as good as they are going to get. Banking on improvement over the holding period is not the basis of prudent investing.

- Is it reasonable to expect property values to rise by 10% annually when rents and expenses are rising by 5%? Is it reasonable to expect that expenses will rise at the same rate as rents? Like automobiles, housing requires more repairs with age. So it is appropriate to expect repairs to rise a bit faster than rents, especially after the honeymoon period of a new property is over when the builder's warranty expires.

- Recast your expectations at more reasonable terms that are likely to occur.

What exactly is "house flipping" and can you make money doing it?

During the recent housing boom, "flipping" became popular. The term refers to buying real estate with the intention of selling it for a profit within a short time span. Often, but not always, the investor will do some amount of fixing up to make the property more appealing to buyers. Under the right conditions, the investor can make stunning gains on a successful flip, hence its popularity.

Why does it sometimes work? A buyer can take advantage of inefficiencies in the market by finding a property that does not attract buyers and turning it around. This may require changing the financing: finding a situation where an owner has gotten in over his head and buying out his interest. Or it might require some financing by the investor. Often the flipper looks for homes whose market appeal can be significantly enhanced through a few cosmetic improvements, ones that buyers might not have the imagination to make on their own.

Flipping usually requires that the demand for real estate be very strong. You do not want to do this in a buyer's market. It requires the investor to know the local market and which neighborhoods are the most in demand, yet still have property that can be had for a relatively good price. The investor must also have a feel for what improvements will make the most difference at the least cost (and have a reliable contractor to do the work). Overall, the technique can work only in special situations. Normally, the high costs of buying and selling real property work against short-term profits.

Can I get in and get out fast?

Prices for real estate fluctuate, but there is no daily stock market report to give you the signal that the party is over. No one rings the bell to signal a time to sell. Even if you have the foresight to anticipate that the bubble will soon burst, it may be difficult or impossible to find a buyer for your property in a short enough period of time to avoid the loss. Keep in mind that real estate can be like a mousetrap—easy to get into, impossible to get out of. You can offer property for sale, but you can't make someone buy it.

Can I lose more than I invest?

Some people think that the worst that can happen is that they can abandon their contract to purchase units under construction and lose only their investment. Or that they can walk away from the units they bought and leave the keys in the mailbox. In most situations, this is not possible. The lender or developer who pre-sold to you does not want just the property back—he will seek to enforce the contract. Unless you have exculpation in the contract (the lender's only recourse is to the property), you will be liable beyond what you paid for the unit. Those who have no assets beyond this property may be able to take bankruptcy to end their losses. Perhaps foreign investors feel that they will be difficult for U.S. lenders to reach. Those who have other assets are vulnerable. So before entering into a contract, it is essential to understand the potential liability for losses, which can far exceed the investment.

GLOSSARY

Accommodator *see* QUALIFIED INTERMEDIARY.

Additional first-year depreciation (tax) in the year 2011 and thereafter, up to $25,000 of depreciable personal property purchased each year may be expensed, rather than depreciated. Generally, this is *not* available for use in buildings or income-producing real estate such as rental or investment property.

Adjusted tax basis the original cost or other basis of property, reduced by DEPRECIATION TAX DEDUCTIONS and increased by capital expenditures.

After-tax cash flow CASH FLOW from income-producing property, less income taxes, if any, attributable to the property's income. If there is a tax loss that can provide a tax savings from the shelter of income earned outside the property, that savings is added to the cash flow that is earned by the property.

Appraisal an opinion or estimate of the value of a property, generally to:

- determine a reasonable offering price in a sale
- determine the value at death for real estate tax purposes
- allocate the purchase price to the land and improvements
- determine the amount of hazard insurance to carry

At-risk rules tax laws that limit the amount of tax losses an investor (particularly a limited partner) can claim. At-risk rules were extended to real estate by the 1986 tax act, and apply to property placed in service after 1986. This means that losses on real estate investments will be deductible only to the extent of money the equity investor stands to lose.

Balloon payment the final payment on a loan, when that payment is greater than the preceding installment payments and pays the loan in full.

Blue-sky laws state laws requiring the offeror of securities to give full disclosure, and register the offering as required by federal and state law.

Break-even point the amount of rent or the occupancy level needed to pay OPERATING EXPENSES and debt service. Also called default point.

$$\text{Break-even point} = \frac{\text{Operating expenses and debt service}}{\text{Potential GROSS INCOME}}$$

Capital asset an asset defined in Section 1221 of the Internal Revenue Code that once received favorable tax treatment upon sale. Excludes inventory, property held for resale, property used in a trade or business, copyrights in certain instances, and certain U.S. government obligations.

Capitalization rate a rate of return used to derive the capital value of an income stream. The formula is:

$$\text{Value} = \frac{\text{Annual income}}{\text{Capitalization rate}}$$

Capture rate the sale or leasing rate of a real estate development compared to the sales or leasing rate of all developments in the market area.

Cash flow periodic amounts available to an equity investor after deducting all periodic cash payments from rental income.

Closing costs various fees and expenses payable by the seller and buyer at the time of a real estate closing (also termed transaction costs).

   Examples: The following are some closing costs:

- brokerage commissions
- lender discount points/other fees
- title insurance premium
- deed recording fees
- loan prepayment penalty
- inspection and appraisal fees
- attorney's fees

Closing statement an accounting of funds from a real estate sale, made to both the seller and the buyer separately. Most states require the broker to furnish accurate closing statements to all parties to the transaction.

Commercial property property designed for use by retail, wholesale, office, hotel, or service users.

194

Cost approach a method of appraising property based on the depreciated reproduction or replacement cost (new) of improvements, plus the MARKET VALUE of the site.

Debt coverage ratio the relationship between net operating income (NOI) and annual debt service (ADS). Often used as an underwriting criterion for income property mortgage loans.

Deficiency judgment a court order stating that the borrower still owes money when the security for a loan does not entirely satisfy a defaulted debt.

Depreciable real estate (tax) realty that is subject to deductions for DEPRECIATION. It generally includes property used in a trade or business, or an investment, subject to an allowance for depreciation under Section 167 of the Internal Revenue Code.

Depreciation (appraisal) a charge against the reproduction cost (new) of an asset for the estimated wear and obsolescence. Depreciation may be physical, functional, or economic.

Discounted cash flow a method of INVESTMENT ANALYSIS in which anticipated future cash income from the investment is estimated and converted into a rate of return on initial investment based on the time value of money. In addition, when a required rate of return is specified, a net present value of the investment can be estimated.

Discount rate 1. a compound interest rate used to convert expected future income into a present value. 2. the rate charged member banks who borrow from the Federal Reserve Bank.

Equity the interest or value that the owner has in real estate over and above the liens against it. The formula is:

Market value	$100,000
Liens	− 60,000
Equity	$ 40,000

Exchange under Section 1031 of the Internal Revenue Code, like-kind property used in a trade or business or held as an investment can be exchanged tax-free.

Exchange-traded fund (ETF) a closed-end pool of real estate whose shares trade on the stock exchange in the manner of individual stocks.

Exculpatory clause a provision in a MORTGAGE allowing the borrower to surrender the property to the lender without personal liability for the loan.

Facilitator *see* QUALIFIED INTERMEDIARY.

195

Feasibility study a determination of the likelihood that a proposed development will fulfill the objectives of a particular investor. A feasibility study of a proposed subdivision should:

- estimate the demand for housing units in the area
- estimate the absorption rate for the project
- discuss legal and other considerations
- forecast CASH FLOWS
- approximate investment returns likely to be produced

Fixtures improvements or personal property attached to the land so as to become part of the real estate. Tests to determine whether an item is a fixture include:

- intent of the parties (was it intended to remain?)
- method of annexation (how is it affixed?)
- relation of the parties (was it expected to be part of a tenant's business?)
- adaptation of the article (is it essential to the building?)

Front foot a standard measurement of land, applied at the frontage of its street line. Used for lots of generally uniform depth in downtown areas.

Gross lease a lease of property whereby the landlord (lessor) is responsible for paying all property expenses, such as taxes, INSURANCE, utilities, and repairs.

Gross profit ratio in an installment sale, the relationship between the gross profit (gain) and the contract price. The resulting fraction is applied to periodic receipts from the buyer to determine the taxable gain from each receipt.

Gross rent multiplier (GRM) the sales price divided by the contract rental rate.

Highest and best use an APPRAISAL term meaning the legally and physically possible use that, at the time of appraisal, is most likely to produce the greatest net return to the land and/or buildings over a given period.

Illiquid an asset that is difficult to convert to cash at its market value, with speed or ease.

Income approach a method appraising real estate based on the property's anticipated future income. The formula for appraisal by the income approach is:

$$\frac{\text{Expected annual income}}{\text{Capitalization rate}} = \text{MARKET VALUE}$$

Index 1. a statistic that indicates some current economic or financial condition. Indexes are often used to make adjustments in wage rates, rental rates, loan interest rates, and pension benefits set by long-term contracts. 2. to adjust contract terms according to an index.

Industrial property property used for industrial purposes, such as factories. Types of industrial property:

- factory-office multiuse property
- factory-warehouse multiuse property
- heavy manufacturing buildings
- industrial parks
- light manufacturing buildings
- research and development parks

Installment sale when a seller accepts a MORTGAGE for part of the sale, the tax on the gain is paid as the mortgage principal is collected.

Interim financing a loan, including a construction loan, used when the property owner is unable or unwilling to arrange permanent financing. Generally arranged for less than 3 years, used to gain time for financial or market conditions to improve.

Internal rate of return (IRR) the true annual rate of earnings on an investment. Equates the value of cash returns with cash invested. Considers the application of compound interest factors. Requires a trial-and-error method for solution. The formula is:

$$\sum_{t=1}^{n} \frac{\text{Periodic cash flow}}{(1 + i)^t} = \text{Investment amount}$$

where i = internal rate of return
t = each time interval
n = total time intervals
Σ = summation

Investment analysis a study of the likely return from a proposed real estate investment with the objective of evaluating the amount an investor may pay for it, the investment's suitability to that investor, or the feasibility of a proposed real estate development. Appraised value is based on a synthesis of people in the market whereas investment analysis is based on the value to a specific investor.

There are various methods of investment analysis, including:

- Cash on cash return
- Payback period
- Internal rate of return
- Net present value

Joint and several liability a creditor can demand full repayment from any and all of those who have borrowed. Each borrower is liable for the full debt, not just the prorated share.

Joint venture an agreement between 2 or more parties who invest in a single business or property.

Lease a contract in which, for a payment called rent, the one entitled to the possession of real property (lessor) transfers those rights to another (lessee) for a specified period of time.

Leverage use of borrowed funds to increase purchasing power and, ideally, to increase the profitability of an investment.

Limited liability the restriction of one's potential losses to the amount invested. The absence of personal liability.

Limited liability company (LLC or LC) either a limited liability corporation (also abbreviated LC or LLC) or a limited liability partnership (LLP). These entities emerged in a few states in the early 1990s. By the mid-1990s, most states adopted legislation allowing them. An LLC or LLP may provide the possibility of federal taxation as a partnership (a flow-through entity that itself normally pays no tax), while all of the owners (who are corporate stockholders in an LLC or partners in an LLP) generally enjoy limited liability. Thus, a limited liability corporation, even though it provides many characteristics of a corporation, may be taxed as a partnership (flow-through) for federal income tax purposes. A limited liability partnership may also be taxed as a partnership although it may offer many corporate characteristics. Unlike a limited partnership, which must have at least one general partner with unlimited liability, none of an LLP's owners must have general liability. However, state law may extend protection by the limited liability to only certain events and may apply unfavorable taxation at the state level.

Because of flexibility in selecting which tax entity to use, combined with the absence of personal liability for all owners, these entities emerged as the favored vehicles for owning real estate in many situations that previously used sole proprietorship, partnership, limited partnership, or Sub S forms. However, you should check state law to determine the extent of liability protection and the method of state taxation.

Limited partnership one in which there is at least one partner who is passive and limits liability to the amount invested, and at least one partner whose liability extends beyond monetary investment.

Liquidity the speed and ease of converting an asset or investment to cash at its market value.

Loan-to-value ratio (L/V) the portion of the amount borrowed compared to the cost or value of the property purchased.

Market analysis a study of the supply and demand conditions in a specific area for a specific property or service. A MARKET ANALYSIS report is generally prepared by someone with experience in real estate, economics, or marketing. It serves to help decide what type of project to develop and is also helpful in arranging permanent and construction financing for a proposed development.

Market comparison approach one of 3 appraisal approaches. Value is estimated by analyzing sales prices of similar properties (comparables) recently sold.

Market value the theoretical highest price a buyer, willing but not compelled to buy, would pay, and the lowest price a seller, willing but not compelled to sell, would accept.

Master limited partnership an ownership vehicle, especially used for real estate or oil and gas ventures. It is generally formed by a "roll up" of existing limited PARTNERSHIPS that own property, and typically has the advantage of ownership interests that are more marketable than individual limited partnerships.

Material participation a tax term introduced by the 1986 tax act, defined as year-round active involvement in the operations of a business activity on a regular, continuous and substantial basis. One with *material participation* may be allowed to deduct certain losses against other income. Three main factors to consider in determining the presence of material participation are:

- Is the activity the taxpayer's principal trade or business?
- How close is the taxpayer to the business?
- Does the taxpayer have knowledge and experience in the enterprise?

Mortgage constant the percentage ratio between the annual debt service and the loan principal. The formula is:

$$\frac{\text{Annual debt service}}{\text{Loan principal}} = \text{Mortgage constant}$$

Negative cash flow situation in which a property owner must make an outlay of funds to operate a property.

Net leasable area in a building or project, floor space that may be rented to tenants. The area upon which rental payments are based. Generally excludes common areas and space devoted to the heating, cooling, and other equipment of a building.

Net lease a lease whereby, in addition to the rent stipulated, the lessee (tenant) pays such expenses as taxes, insurance, and maintenance. The landlord's rent receipt is thereby "net" of those expenses.

Net operating income (NOI) income from property or business after OPERATING EXPENSES have been deducted, but before deducting income taxes and financing expenses (interest and principal payments).

Nonrecourse no personal liability. Lenders may take the property pledged as collateral to satisfy a debt, but have no recourse to other assets of the borrower.

Obsolescence a loss in value due to reduced desirability and usefulness of a structure because its design and construction has become obsolete; loss due to a structure's becoming old-fashioned, not in keeping with modern needs, with consequent loss of income.

Overall rate of return (OAR) the percentage relationship of net operating income divided by the purchase price of property.

Partnership an agreement between two or more entities to go into business or invest. Either partner may bind the other, within the scope of the PARTNERSHIP. Each partner is liable for all the partnership's debts. A partnership normally pays no taxes, but merely files an information return. The individual partners pay personal income tax on their share of income.

Passive activity income under the 1986 tax act, is generated by: 1. any trade or business conducted for profit in which the taxpayer does not materially participate. 2. any rental activity, whether or not the taxpayer materially participates.

Rental activities are presumed to be passive. These include all activities that generate income from payments for the use of property rather than for the performance of services. Rental activities include long-term rentals of apartments, net leased property, office equipment, and automobiles. In contrast, the rental of hotel rooms or transient apartments and short-term car rentals are not passive because of the extent of services provided.

Passive income 1. generally, income from rents, royalties, dividends, interest, and gains from the sale of securities. 2. a new meaning created by the Tax Reform Act of 1986 distinguishes passive income or loss from active income and portfolio income.

Payback period the amount of time required for cumulative estimated future income from an investment to equal the amount initially invested. It is used to compare alternative investment opportunities.

Percentage lease a lease of property in which the rental is based on a percentage of the volume of sales made upon the leased premises. It usually stipulates a minimum rental and is regularly used for retailers who are tenants.

Portfolio income interest, dividends, royalties (unless earned in the ordinary course of business) and gains from the sale or property that generates this type of income. Under the Tax Reform Act of 1986 this type of income cannot be used to offset passive activity losses. See **passive income.**

Potential gross income the amount of income that could be produced by a real property assuming no vacancies or collection losses. Does not include miscellaneous income.

Prime rate the lowest commercial interest rate charged by banks on short-term loans to their most credit-worthy customers. The prime rate is not the same as the long-term mortgage rate, though it may influence the long-term rates. Also, it is not the same as the consumer loan rate that is charged on personal property loans and credit cards. Mortgage rates and consumer loan rates are generally higher than the prime rate, but exceptions occur at times.

Prime tenant in a shopping center or office building, the tenant who occupies the most space. Prime tenants are considered credit-worthy and attract customers or traffic to the center.

Private offering an investment or business offered for sale to a small group of investors, generally under exemptions to registration allowed by the Securities and Exchange Commission and state securities registration laws.

Pro-forma statement according to form. Financial statements showing what is expected to occur.

Prospectus a printed descriptive statement about a business or investment that is for sale, to invite the interest of prospective investors.

Public offering soliciting the general public for the sale of investment units. Generally requires approval by the SEC and/or state securities agencies. Contrast with **private offering.**

Qualified intermediary a person or entity that can legally hold funds to facilitate a Section 1031 exchange. Such an intermediary is usually needed to complete a delayed exchange. To be qualified, the intermediary must not be a relative or agent of the exchanging party. As an exception, a real estate agent may serve as intermediary if the current transaction is the only instance in which the agent has represented the exchanging party over the past two years.

Real estate investment trust (REIT) a real estate mutual fund, allowed by income tax laws to avoid the corporate income tax. It sells shares of ownership and must invest in real estate or MORTGAGES. It must meet certain other requirements, including minimum number of shareholders, widely dispersed ownership, asset and income tests. If it distributes 95% of its income to shareholders, it is not taxed on that income, but shareholders must include their share of the REIT's income in their personal tax returns.

Real estate mortgage investment conduit (REMIC) The purpose of a REMIC is to hold a fixed pool of mortgages and issue interests in itself to mortgage investors. A REMIC may be a partnership, corporation, trust, or separate pool of assets. REMICs are intended to become the exclusive means for issuing multiple-class mortgage-backed securities in a form that avoids the corporate double tax.

Rehabilitation tax credit the Tax Reform Act of 1986 provides a 20% tax credit for rehabilitating certified historic structures, and a 10% credit for other buildings that were placed in service after 1936. However, there are certain conditions or requirements that are imposed.

Release clause in a MORTGAGE, a clause that gives the owner of the property the privilege of paying off a portion of the mortgage indebtedness, thus freeing a portion of the property from the mortgage.

Reserve fund an account maintained to provide funds for anticipated expenditures required to maintain a building. A reserve may be required by a lender in the form of an escrow to pay upcoming taxes and insurance costs. A replacement reserve may be maintained to provide for replacement cost of short-lived components, such as carpets, heating equipment, or roofing. Deposit of money into such a fund does not achieve a tax deduction.

Retail gravitation the drawing power of a shopping center; generally, the larger the center, the greater its ability to draw from distant areas.

Retainage in a construction contract, money earned by a contractor but not paid to the contractor until the completion of construction or some other agreed-upon date.

Risk 1. uncertainty or variability. The possibility that returns from an investment will be greater or less than forecast. Diversification of investments provides some protection against RISK. 2. the possibility of a loss. INSURANCE can offer protection against certain risks.

S corporation a corporation with a limited number of stockholders (75 or fewer) that elects not to be taxed as a regular corporation, and meets certain other requirements. Shareholders include, in their personal tax return, their pro-rata share of CAPITAL GAINS, ordinary income, tax preference items, and so on. See **passive income.**

Sale-leaseback the simultaneous purchase of property and leaseback to the seller. The lease portion of the transaction is generally long-term. The seller-lessee in the transaction is converted from an owner to a tenant.

Securitization the process of creating a security marketable in the capital markets and backed by a package of assets such as mortgage loans.

Sensitivity analysis a technique of INVESTMENT ANALYSIS whereby different values of certain key variables are tested to see how sensitive investment results are to possible change in assumptions. It is a method of evaluating the riskiness of an investment.

Standby loan a commitment by a lender to make available a sum of money at specified terms for a specific period. A standby fee is charged for this commitment. The borrower retains the option of choosing the loan or allowing the commitment to lapse.

Stepped-up basis an income tax term used to describe a change in the adjusted tax basis of property, allowed for certain transactions. The old basis is increased to MARKET VALUE upon inheritance, as opposed to a carry-over basis in the event of a tax-free exchange.

Stop clause in a lease, stipulates an amount of OPERATING EXPENSE above which the tenant must bear. Often the base amount is the amount of expense for the first full year of operation under the lease.

Straight-line depreciation equal annual reductions in the book value of property. It is used in accounting for replacement and tax purposes.

Syndication a method of selling property whereby a sponsor (or syndicator) sells interests to investors. May take the form of a PARTNERSHIP, limited partnership, tenancy in common, corporation, LLC or LLP, or S Corporation.

Take-out financing a commitment to provide permanent financing following construction of a planned project. The take-out commitment is generally predicted upon specific conditions, such as a certain percentage of unit sales or leases, for the permanent loan to "take out" the construction loan. Most construction lenders require take-out financing.

Tax shelter an investment that produces after-tax income that is greater than before-tax income. The investment may produce before-tax CASH FLOW while generating losses to shield, from taxation, income from sources outside the investment.

Tenancy in common an ownership of realty by 2 or more persons, each of whom has an undivided interest, without the right of survivorship. Upon the death of one of the owners, the ownership share of the decedent is inherited by the party or parties designated in the decedent's will.

Vacancy rate the percentage of all units or space that is unoccupied or not rented. On a pro-forma income statement a projected vacancy rate is used to estimate the vacancy allowance, which is deducted from POTENTIAL GROSS INCOME to derive EFFECTIVE GROSS INCOME.

Workout a mutual effort by a property owner and lender to avoid foreclosure or bankruptcy following a default; generally involves substantial reduction in the debt service burden during an economic depression.

Wraparound mortgage a loan arrangement in which an existing loan is retained and an additional loan, larger than the existing loan, is made. The new lender who receives the monthly payment accepts the obligation to make payments on the old loan. The existing loan generally carries an interest rate below the rate available on new loans. Consequently, the yield to the wraparound lender is higher than the rate charged on the new loan. Sellers are the most common wraparound lenders.

Yield 1. a measurement of the rate of earnings from an investment. 2. the productivity of agricultural land.

INDEX

NOTES

NOTES

More selected BARRON'S titles:

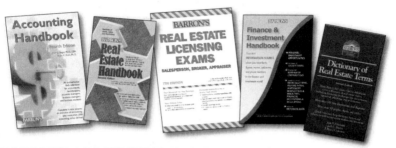

BARRON'S ACCOUNTING HANDBOOK, 4th ED.
Joel G. Siegel and Jae K. Shim
Provides accounting rules, guidelines, formulas and techniques, etc. to help students and
business professionals work out accounting problems.
ISBN 978-0-7641-5776-5, 880 pages

REAL ESTATE HANDBOOK, 7th ED.
Jack P. Friedman, Jack C. Harris, and Barry A. Diskin
A dictionary/reference for everyone in real estate. Defines approximately 2000 legal,
financial, and architectural terms.
ISBN 978-0-7641-6110-0, approx. 784 pages

REAL ESTATE LICENSING EXAMS: SALESPERSON, BROKER, APPRAISER, 7th ED.
J. Bruce Lindeman and Jack P. Friedman
Reviews current exam topics and features updated model exams and supplemental exams,
all with explained answers.
ISBN 978-0-7641-2402-0, 340 pages

BARRON'S FINANCE AND INVESTMENT HANDBOOK, 7th ED.
John Downes and Jordan Elliot Goodman
This hard-working handbook of essential information defines more than 3000 key terms,
and explores 30 basic investment opportunities. The investment information is thoroughly
up-to-date.
ISBN 978-0-7641-5992-3, 1408 pages

DICTIONARY OF REAL ESTATE TERMS, 7th ED.
Jack P. Friedman, Jack C. Harris, and J. Bruce Lindeman
This valuable handbook for home buyers and sellers defines and explains approximately
3000 real estate terms related to mortgages and financing, brokerage law, architecture,
rentals and leases, property insurance, and much more.
ISBN 978-0-7641-3936-9, 560 pages

Barron's Educational Series, Inc.
250 Wireless Blvd., Hauppauge, NY 11788
In Canada: Georgetown Book Warehouse
34 Armstrong Ave., Georgetown, Ontario L7G 4R9

Please visit **www.barronseduc.com** to
view current prices and to order books

NOTES

--

--

Northbrook Public Library
(847) 272-6224
www.northbrook.info

User name: Erickson, Charles W.

Call number: 332.6324 FIS
Title: The real estate investor's handbook
 : the complet
Item ID: 31123008183223
Date due: 8/8/2012,23:59

Call number: 332.6324 FRI
Title: Keys to investing in real estate
Item ID: 31123009522866
Date due: 8/8/2012,23:59

M-Th 9-9,Fr 9-6,Sa 9-5,Su 1-5
-- -- -- -- -- -- -- -- -- --
Summer Reading Clubs!
for Adults and Youths
Join beginning June 1
-----   -----

NOTES

The Smart Consumer's Guide to Home Buying

Peter A. Schkeeper, Licensed Engineer, Jack P. Friedman, Ph.D., CPA, MAI, CRE, ASA, and Jack C. Harris, Ph.D.

Buying a home is—in the authors' words—both a romantic journey and a business venture. For most families, it's the largest single investment they will ever make. The purpose of this book is to transform home buyers—especially first-time buyers—into smart consumers who can evaluate a property objectively as step number one in deciding whether or not to buy. The authors take their readers by the hand through the maze of mortgage shopping, dealing with real estate agents, and hunting down that perfect dream house. Some of the many questions they help prospective buyers answer are—

- Consideration of family needs: how many rooms, what kind of neighborhood, access to schools, shopping, and the like
- Is the home affordable? Considerations include the size of the down payment, the size and type of mortgage, projecting monthly payments, and allowing for unforeseen expenses
- Making an offer and negotiating with sellers and real estate agents
- The close, settlement, and escrow
- Remodeling: adding to a home and making improvements
- Investment Property: understanding market values
- Selling a home . . . and much, much more

Because this book addresses a national audience, it is necessarily general when making reference to local situations. However, the authors offer practical advice on how readers can find reliable local professional assistance in their quest to purchase a home.

Paperback, 528 pp., ISBN-13: 978-0-7641-3571-2

Please visit **www.barronseduc.com** to view current prices and to order books

Barron's Educational Series, Inc.
250 Wireless Blvd.
Hauppauge, NY 11788
Order toll-free: 1-800-645-3476
Order by fax: 1-631-434-3217

In Canada:
Georgetown Book Warehouse
34 Armstrong Ave.
Georgetown, Ont. L7G 4R9
Canadian orders: 1-800-247-7160
Fax in Canada: 1-800-887-1594

(#162) R 5/08